COUNTRY SCHOOL
MEMORIES

COUNTRY SCHOOL MEMORIES

An Oral History of
One-Room Schooling

ROBERT L. LEIGHT
ALICE DUFFY RINEHART

Contributions to the Study of Education, Number 74

GREENWOOD PRESS
Westport, Connecticut • London

Library of Congress Cataloging-in-Publication Data

Leight, Robert L., 1932–
     Country school memories : an oral history of one-room schooling /
  Robert L. Leight, Alice Duffy Rinehart.
        p. cm.—(Contributions to the study of education, ISSN
  0196–707X ; no. 74)
     Includes bibliographical references (p.   ) and index.
     ISBN 0–313–30919–1 (alk. paper)
     1. Rural schools—Pennsylvania—History—20th century—Case
  studies. 2. Education, Rural—Pennsylvania—History—20th century—
  Case studies. 3. Teachers—Pennsylvania—Interviews. 4. Students—
  Pennsylvania—Interviews. 5. Oral history. I. Rinehart, Alice
  Duffy. II. Title. III. Series.
  LC5147.P4L45   1999
  370′.91734—dc21   98–41417

British Library Cataloguing in Publication Data is available.

Library of Congress Catalog Card Number: 98–41417
ISBN: 0–313–30919–1
ISSN: 0196–707X

First published in 1999

Greenwood Press, 88 Post Road West, Westport, CT 06881
An imprint of Greenwood Publishing Group, Inc.

Printed in the United States of America

The paper used in this book complies with the
Permanent Paper Standard issued by the National
Information Standards Organization (Z39.48–1984).

10 9 8 7 6 5 4 3 2 1

Ode to a Little Red Schoolhouse

Little schoolhouse on the hill,
Toll your bell, time stands not still.
Bless you as we close your door,
And bless the days that come no more.
Rememb'ring now the books we read,
The songs we sang, the things we said.
The science corner, water pail,
Great black stove, exciting mail.
Outside "bathrooms," drafty, chill,
And belly-flopping down the hill.
Hiking in the woods in spring,
Wonderment in everything—
Mary, six, and Bill, sixteen,
And forty others in between—
Living, learning every day,
From harvest time to merry May.
Little school, your work is done,
Ring your bell for laurels won.

—Margaret M. Seylar

(Read at groundbreaking of the East Rockhill Consolidated School, May 1956. Margaret Seylar was the supervising principal of the Deep Run Valley School District.)

Contents

Illustrations

An old country school. This is the former Shelly School, which has been preserved by the Richland (One-Room School) Historical Society. Many of the persons interviewed for this study are members of the society. The building is of red brick, and it is fondly called "The Little Red Schoolhouse." Photo reproduced courtesy of the Quakertown Community School District.

Preface

Often, we do not fully appreciate old friends until they are gone. We ignore the familiar, taking for granted the very comforts that serve us well.

That certainly seems to be true of an institution that was very familiar in rural America until about a half-century ago, the little country school. From almost the turn of the century these small places were marked for extinction, deemed by experts to be inferior to the "modern" specialized schools of the city and suburbs. Once the educational policymakers determined that they would be replaced by consolidated schools, almost no one tried to save them. By the 1920s, they were going fast.

Those schoolhouses that were not replaced by 1930 got an uncertain reprieve, for there was no money to build schoolhouses during the Great Depression, and no resources that could be spared for school buildings during World War II. But with the baby boom of the 1950s, together with an increasingly urbanized and industrialized society, it was felt that country people needed the same modern schools as the cities, and the little schools were abandoned.

Now that they are gone, they are missed. Some of these old friends are still standing, although they are serving other purposes. But country people retain vivid memories of their childhood, and an older rural generation still recalls the old one-room and two-room schools.

We decided to tap the rich storehouses of memory held by some of those who had attended little country schools as teachers or pupils. This book is the product of those probes into long-term memories of the one-room school experience by means of audiotaped interviews.

It took a long time to get the book organized and written. Both of us had careers and other responsibilities that got in the way of reaching closure. We began our first interviews in 1986, and did not finish the book until 1998. But it has been a labor of love.

The forty-seven persons who consented to share their memories of school days are vibrant people, who were generous in their sharing and open in their comments. As many were elderly when interviewed, a substantial proportion of them have passed away during the long period in which the book was created. We are thankful that their memories exist in our tapes and transcripts. We express appreciation to all of those who consented to interviews, and wish that we could have included even more of their memories on these pages.

Although our subjects are or were our neighbors, we believe that the experiences that they described are fairly representative of the thousands of people who shared the one-room school experience in various parts of the country during the first half of the twentieth century.

We wish to thank Lehigh University for its support of the research, and particularly to express our thanks to the extraordinary secretary who helped to put this book into its final form, Donna Toothman.

The One-Room, One-Teacher School

For almost 250 years the country school was the backbone of American education. As late as 1913, one-half of the schoolchildren in the United States were enrolled in the country's 212,000 one room-schools. . . . Only about 835 of these one-teacher, one-room schools, or .05 percent of all public school buildings, remain in use today.
—Andrew Gulliford (*America's Country Schools,* 1991, 31)

Rural schools are a part of American tradition. The current study was undertaken in order to preserve some of their history from participants before it is forgotten. Included are the results of interviews with forty-seven participants in one- or two-room schools, primarily in the northern part of Bucks County, Pennsylvania, which was mainly rural until mid-twentieth century.

During the nineteenth century a network of small country schools was built throughout the nation. Many of these schools had just one teacher teaching eight grades in one room. These schools were numerous in agricultural states; Pennsylvania had many of them in rural areas. But they disappeared more rapidly than they originally appeared. In the decade following World War II, they were virtually eliminated in a movement to modernize elementary education as the process of school consolidation was completed.

These little schools have disappeared forever, swept away by the tides of school reform. Where once there were thousands of small schools dotting the American rural landscape as late as the 1950s, they have now vanished, except in very remote areas or as parochial schools, such as for the Amish or conservative Mennonites of Pennsylvania. In terms of historical perspective, this transition is remarkable, as for more than one hundred years the small school was almost the only form of rural elementary education. In fact, even in urban areas until the Civil War the one-teacher school was predominant.

The schools are gone, but many of the original buildings remain. They are now artifacts, reminding us that they were once alive with the sounds of children learning and teachers teaching. Most of those built after the Civil War were constructed on standard architectural designs, and they were built to last. As one travels through the rural countryside, and even in some suburban communities, the distinctively simple, rectangular buildings can still be found by those who look for them. Many have been remodeled into homes, but others are used as country stores or meeting houses. A few have been preserved almost as they were when last filled with children fifty years ago. Time has mellowed perceptions of them, but, as Gulliford has noted, there is still an ambiguity in the conventional wisdom about these little schools.

Perceptions of American country schools are clouded by two contradictory myths. One is that country schools are the poor stepchildren of American education— primitive buildings where, under intolerable conditions, young, inexperienced teachers try to instill in their students a modicum of knowledge. Another is the myth of the little red schoolhouse pleasantly situated beneath shade trees and full of bright, young students eager to learn their lessons and please their teacher. Neither view is wholly true nor wholly false. In some country schools, discipline was lax and learning incidental, but other schools were orderly, efficient and staunchly supported by the community, offering children an opportunity for education that few of their parents had enjoyed. (Gulliford, 1991, 35)

These small country schools fit the values and aspirations of rural America. Until the twentieth century, America was still primarily a rural country. In the Northeast and Midwest, the idea of free public education had been almost universally accepted by 1850, and the tide swept westward with the frontier. The ideology of public education took root in the heyday of Jacksonian democracy. A community school responsive to the needs and within the resources of a local community and pretty much controlled by elected school directors became the linchpin of public education. One-room schools flowered.

In rural Pennsylvania the boundaries of school districts were coterminous with those of the townships. The township school boards generally built one-room schools and spread them out so that they were accessible by foot travel by the children of the township. The schoolhouses were usually standardized both in size and physical layout. Some were built with wood siding, some of local stone, and some of brick (the little red schoolhouse). If the community wanted to do something extra to dress up the schoolhouse it added a steeple with a bell. Indeed, many of the schoolhouses served double duty as union Sunday schools, so the churchlike appearance of those with bell towers was appropriate.

By current standards, the school yards were very small. At most, the school had a half-acre plot as it was situated next to a country road. On that plot sat two outside toilets, one for boys and one for girls, and sometimes other outbuildings such as coal and wood bins. The students either had to invent games that could be played on the small playgrounds or to infiltrate the neighboring farmer's pasture, crop fields, or wood lot to find additional space in which to play.

Although the conventional wisdom of the nineteenth century was that male teachers were needed to master the unruly boys, women teachers had proven themselves when the male teachers had been called to serve in the Civil War. By the 1920s and 1930s women teachers predominated in elementary education in general, and in country schools in particular. Wages were so low that a male breadwinner needed to find a more remunerative occupation. There was, however, a fair number of young men who taught for a few years to earn money and maturity before moving on to another profession. Some males were discouraged by the lack of job security. Many of the women teachers were the traditional "old-maid schoolmarms." After World War I, many of the better-paying school districts did not hire married female teachers, whereas the rural school districts did not have the luxury of restricting this excellent labor pool.

Until World War I one could begin to teach with minimal preparation, with as little as a summer course between high school and the first year of teaching. But by the 1930s and 1940s the "normal schools," which specialized in preparing entry-level teachers, had been transformed into four-year state teachers colleges. By then it was fairly typical for a young teacher to gain a teaching certificate by going to a teachers college or taking brief teacher training courses at a liberal arts college, and then to be hired to teach while still in her late teens or early twenties. If she liked teaching and was successful and did not marry, she might well have a career of forty or more years, sometimes in the same schoolhouse. Those who married and had children tended to drop out of teaching to be career mothers until their children were older, although they might do some substitute teaching or tutoring. When their children were in high school or working at jobs these former teachers would often return to the classroom in their thirties or forties for a second tour of teaching.

The one-room school could become almost a self-contained miniature society. A single adult spent long days in the company of a multi-aged group of children. Sometimes the children were as young as five; while the eighth-graders were already young adolescents.

These mini-societies were often quite isolated. There were no other adults than the teacher. She was the instructor, counselor, nurse, disciplinarian, and custodian. In addition, she was responsible for contacts with the homes of the children. These teachers were the general practitioners of education. They were also parent substitutes. In several cases, those interviewed spoke of the people in the schoolroom as a "family." The classmates were like siblings. Sometimes they were indeed brothers and sisters, for there would often be two, three, even four children from the same family in the one schoolroom.

Each isolated school was a world of face-to-face, long-lasting relationships. There was no visible bureaucracy. The classroom teacher was engaged with children all day, except for a temporary respite when the students were at recess or lunch. Such teachers had the potential to have an enormous influence, especially if they stayed at the same school or taught in the same community for long careers.

A child who had passed through one of these schools in the first decades of the twentieth century would find a familiar environment if he or she returned at midcentury. Textbooks would have changed; the slang and clothing styles certainly would be different, but the teachers' techniques and the physical setting would have changed very little. The most important visual aid would still have been slate blackboards. Routines were similar at mid-century to those of the early decades. The teachers would still be calling small groups of children "up front" for recitation while the others were doing seat work. The students' desks would have a patina of wear and perhaps the indentations of generations of students' initials traced in them. Probably there was a circular hole in the desktop where an inkwell had sat in earlier days. But the middle-aged adult who looked into the schools in midcentury could easily feel that he or she had entered a time warp. Country schools were institutions of great stability and continuity.

Probably the most noted environmental change would have been that electric lights could be turned on when there were cloudy days or for night programs. Much of rural America was electrified during the 1930s. Most of the unpaved rural roads were paved by 1950. But to the end, most one-room schools did not have indoor plumbing. Many did not even have running water. Although the potbellied stove might have been replaced by a newer, more efficient model, the stove was hand-fired and would still dominate the classroom space.

Each little school was a miniature culture, which was also a subculture of its community. One of the reasons the one-room school lasted so long was that there were organic ties with the rest of rural America. The schools and their small societies were reflections of rural lifestyle and the habits of farmers. For example, although the school day began and ended at specific times, the schedule within the school day was relatively flexible. There were no bells or buzzers that cut into lessons as in today's schools, signaling that it is time to "turn off" reading and "turn on" mathematics, or move to another room. The pacing was slower and controlled by the teacher, rather than by a master schedule. The farms that many of the children came from operated in the same way. The milk truck came to pick up the milk at a specific time, but farmers scheduled their farm chores according to their own pace.

In those pretelevision days the rural schools were often the center of popular culture. Many teachers hoped to improve the level of cultural literacy by scheduling a literary program for Friday afternoon, where the students would sing, recite poems, put on plays, and hold debating contests with their peers. More ambitious than the Friday afternoon literary programs were evening Parent-Teacher Association (PTA) meetings, which showcased the talents of the students in plays, singing, recitations, and other exercises. These programs were designed to highlight the talent of the students and to promote confidence in those shy rural children as they performed before a friendly audience. Many of the PTAs also raised money for the school.

Early in this century, many students dropped out of school to work at farm or factory. But as more of the student body stayed on to the eighth grade, many of the township school systems held graduation exercises as their students departed from the eighth grade. Valedictorians were selected for special recognition based upon the grades earned in class and the score gained in a county-administered comprehensive examination. Commencement exercises demonstrated the pride of the community in those fourteen-year-old scholars who passed the county exam and who were thus sent out into the world of higher education (high school) or to the world of work, armed with an eighth-grade diploma.

The rural schools depended upon a considerable contribution of time through the voluntarism of members of their community. In one case that was described by a former teacher interviewed for this study, a PTA group bought land for a playground for the students. Other parent groups installed electricity, provided transportation for trips to neighboring schools for competitions such as spelling bees and baseball games, and helped to clear the snow from the roads that would be traveled in the winters.

The school boards themselves were composed of unpaid volunteers. Those board members set the taxes, bought the textbooks and instructional supplies, paid the teachers, and ordered coal and wood. Often they performed the routine maintenance of the buildings and grounds. At their best, they were solid supporters of the educational program. At their worst, they were stingy and backward. More often, by far, they were the former.

Not too long ago one-room schools were found almost everywhere in rural Pennsylvania and in some other sections of the country. Now they are gone. Lost forever is the opportunity to study these rural schools as observers or participants. Therefore, we asked a number of individuals who had attended the small country schools of a region in southeastern Pennsylvania to share their recollections of their participation as students, and in some cases, as teachers. Forty-seven of these individuals gave tape-recorded interviews. These interviews were the primary source for this history of rural schooling in southeastern Pennsylvania, spanning the years from the first decade of the twentieth century to the mid-1950s. Life in small, country schools during the first half of the twentieth century will be described by individuals who experienced it. As much as is feasible, we have allowed the participants to tell their stories in their own words. Prior to these oral histories, we examine in more detail the extent and eventual demise of the one-room school.

SCOPE OF THE ONE-ROOM SCHOOL

The process of transition from small country schools to consolidated schools was rapid during the period under study. Pennsylvania in 1931–32 reported 6,511 one-teacher schools. The Keystone State had already seen a considerable amount of school consolidation by the early 1930s, as legislation had been passed as early as 1900, which made school consolidation available as the result of local referenda. Probably the peak numbers of one–teacher schools in Pennsylvania occurred in the period just prior to World War I. Miller reported 10,606 one-room schools in Pennsylvania in 1915. At that time 886 of the schools had less than eleven students each (Miller, 1979, 79).

Although Pennsylvania's school-aged population increased dramatically in the five decades from 1910 to 1960, its one-room, one-teacher schools had decreased in that period from more than 10,000 to only 400. By the mid-1960s the Pennsylvania public one-room schools had virtually all closed.

SCHOOL CONSOLIDATION

Considerable school consolidation took place nationally during the 1920s, resulting in the closing of many small schools. In a report about trends during this period, the U.S. Office of Education reported on the pace in which students and teachers of one-room schools were being sent to consolidated schools across the nation. However, small schools still educated a majority of rural children at the end of the 1920s. A government report states that:

consolidated schools have increased on an average of 1,000 yearly during the past decade. There has been a corresponding annual decrease of five-thousand 1-room schools during the past decade. The 1-room school, with a teacher covering all subjects of the curriculum for the eight elementary grades is still the type of school which most of the children living in rural districts attend. (*Biennial Survey of Education*, 1930, 65)

National Trends

Data on the extent of one-room schools are not very reliable until 1915–16, when the U.S. Office of Education began to gather and report in a consistent fashion information about small country schools in biennial publications. By the 1940s and 1950s, Walter Gaumitz, an official in the Office of Education who specialized in rural education, provided an interpretation of the data. His first analysis was published in 1940, under the title, "Are the One-Teacher Schools Passing?" A decade later, Gaumitz and Blose provided a follow-up report, *The One-Teacher School—Its Midcentury Status* (Gaumitz and Blose, 1950). In this report, several comparisons are made:

In 1917–18 there were in the United States 196,037 one-teacher elementary schools. This sum was 70.8 percent of all of the public schools that year. These one-teacher schools employed 31 percent of all the teachers, and it is estimated that they were attended by about 5 million, or about one-fourth, of all of the children. While data are not available to show the number of pupils transported at public expense in 1917–18, it is known that $7,961,291 was spent for such transportation during the school year in question.

During the school year 1947–48 there were in operation in the United States a total of 74,944 one-teacher schools. This is not only a very large number of schools but 44.2 percent of all of the public schools maintained during that year. . . . [I]n 1948 about a million and a half children depended upon these schools for their educational start in life. Thus, despite the continuous, and sometimes precipitous, decline in the number of schools since 1917–18 (averaging about 4,036 per year or 12 per day) there are still many of them operating in the United States. (Gaumitz and Blose, 1950, 6)

In their summary, Gaumitz and Blose made four points about the one-room schools of the nation at midcentury:

(1)   nationally, over half of these small schools were closed in the 30-year period from 1917–18 to 1947–48,
(2)   the decrease in one-room schools was an indication of the progress of rural school centralization,
(3)   in certain regions, notably the northwestern prairie states, there were still significant numbers of one-teacher schools, and
(4)   with one-and-one-half-million children attending one-teacher schools, they were still a significant part of the American educational system.
                                        (Gaumitz and Blose, 1950, 14–15)

The following are statistics for the continental United States from 1917–18 to 1947–48 (Gaumitz and Blose, 1950, 6):

School Term	Number of One-Teacher Schools
1917–18	196,037
1927–28	156,066
1937–38	121,310
1939–40	113,964
1941–42	107,691
1943–44	96,301
1945–46	86,562
1947–48	74,944

In Pennsylvania, the statistics for the same period are given below (Gaumitz and Blose, 1950, 6):

School Term	Number of One-Teacher Schools
1917–18	9,846
1927–28	7,821
1937–38	5,350
1939–40	4,861
1941–42	4,402
1943–44	4,070
1945–46	3,621
1947–48	2,744

Concurrent with the post–World War II baby boom the pace of school centralization picked up. The following are national figures for the contiguous forty-eight states as reported in the *Biennial Survey of Education in the United States* in the Statistical Summaries of 1951–52 (p. 23) and 1954–56 (p. 26).

School Term	Number of One-Teacher Schools
1949–50	59,652
1951–52	50,742
1953–54	42,965
1955–56	34,964

The 1950s and the early 1960s was a period of intense school construction, as the baby boom generation hit the schools. It was also the beginning of a wave of suburbanization, as a network of interstate highways permitted city workers to move to the new suburbs that circled the cities. The newly constructed schools permitted the closing of virtually all of the small schools by the mid-1960s. But school consolidation added to the cost of education. Not only were there additional costs for specialized teachers and for administrators, there was the additional cost of busing the students to the consolidated schools.

PUPIL TRANSPORTATION

In addition to the capital expense of building new schools, each consolidated school added the expense of transportation. The U.S. Office of Education maintained records on the costs of public school transportation for the contiguous states from 1929–30 to 1957–58. The following table is taken from the *Biennial Survey of Education in the United States* for 1957–58 (1962, Table 19):

School Term	Percent of Pupils Transported	Average Cost per Student
1929–30	7.4	$28.81
1931–32	9.2	$24.01
1933–34	10.6	$19.29
1935–36	12.3	$19.27
1937–38	14.5	$20.07
1939–40	16.3	$20.10
1941–42	18.3	$20.64
1943–44	19.4	$23.88
1945–46	21.7	$25.66
1947–48	24.4	$30.11
1949–50	27.7	$30.86
1951–52	29.0	$34.93
1953–54	32.8	$36.55
1955–56	35.0	$36.51
1957–58	36.5	$38.34

Fluctuations in the average costs of transportation per student can be explained by the effects of the Depression and postwar inflation. But there was essentially an inverse relationship between the number of small country schools closed and the number of students who needed to be transported. These expenditures were significant. In 1929–30 the expenditure of public funds for transportation, excluding the capital outlays for school buses, was about $55 million; by 1957–58 the expenditures were more than $416 million. The U.S. Office of Education provided a comparison of these expenses in its *Biennial Survey of Education in the United States*:

The number and percentage of pupils transported at public expense, and the expenditures for such transportation, have all increased steadily since 1929–30. . . . In 1929–30, 1,903,000 children, or 7 out of each 100 enrolled, were transported at public expense; but in 1957–58, almost 37 percent of the pupils in average daily attendance, or a total of 10,862,000, were provided this service. In addition, 104,000 non-public school pupils were transported at public expense. Expenditures for transportation, excluding capital outlay, were almost eight times as great in 1957–58 as in 1929–30. The increase in pupils transported and in transportation costs is a natural result of the elimination of 1-teacher and other small schools as the consolidation of schools and of administrative units progresses. (1962, 18)

The rush to school consolidation was so great that little notice was paid to the additional costs of public transportation. But by 1958, the public school districts of the nation were spending close to a half-billion dollars to put almost eleven million children on the road to and from the new schools.

WHY DID THE SCHOOLS GO?

Because the rural school is to-day in a state of arrested development, burdened by educational traditions, lacking in effective supervision, controlled largely by rural people, who, too often, do not realize either their own needs or the possibilities of rural education, and taught by teachers who, generally speaking, have but little comprehension of the rural-life problem or of the possibilities of a reorganized and redirected rural school, the task of reorganizing and redirecting rural education is difficult, and will necessarily, be slow. (Cubberly, 1914, 105–6)

Ellwood P. Cubberly was among the many influential policymakers who took aim at rural education in general, and the small schools in particular, in the early decades of the twentieth century. His book, *Rural Life and Education*, was an indictment of all of the institutions of rural America. His strategy of remaking rural schools so they were like the urban schools was largely successful in the long run, for school consolidation used the city schools of the early decades of the twentieth century as the model for the rural consolidated schools of the mid-twentieth century. But school consolidation was just one example of the reorganization of the scale of rural institutions.

Many institutions took root in the nineteenth century and flourished during the first half of the twentieth century in rural America. There were general stores and general farms and general medical practitioners. Most are gone, replaced by supermarkets, agribusinesses, and medical centers staffed by specialists. The one-room, one-teacher school was rooted in the agricultural society of earlier times, as were these other community-based institutions. Specialization was certainly one of the reasons for the demise of the small, country school. But the virtual elimination of them in the decade and a half following the end of World War II has other explanations, as well.

Three factors should be considered as those most instrumental in bringing about the demise of the one-room, one-teacher school:

1. The assessment by educational experts that rural one-room schools were "inferior" to urban schools.
2. The belief that there were greater economies to be gained by consolidation of the smaller schools into multi-grade, multi-room structures.
3. The movement to modernize because of the urbanization of population, as the fulcrum of American economy moved from agriculture to manufacturing, and a political system became world-oriented and no longer isolated as a result of two world wars.

Although these concerns were certainly intertwined, they will be discussed separately below.

The Inferior Status of the One-Teacher, One-Room School

Perhaps the most prevalent educational reform of the decades immediately after the Civil War was the classroom "grading" of students into instructional groups. It became possible to group students by their age and academic level. Graded textbooks, such as the famous McGuffey Readers, permitted the placement of students in appropriate grade levels, even within the one-room schools. In areas of denser population, it was possible to build multi-room school buildings and to place in an eight-room building all of the students who were functioning at approximately the same reading level in a separate room with a separate elementary teacher. Essentially, urban education became "age-graded."

This grouping approach seems natural today, because it is so universally practiced. But graded classrooms were hailed as a major accomplishment in the 1850–90 period in cities and larger towns. In the sparsely populated countryside, the small schools achieved something of the same result by the technique of assigning students by grade level within the single classroom. In some cases, the schoolhouse had two or more rooms. One person whom we interviewed, who then lived in a little town, went to a four-room school, in which there were two grades per room.

There was a status gap between the country schools and the urban schools. By the turn of the twentieth century, the urban schools were staffed by "experts," or specialists, in a variety of education roles. There were building administrators or "principals" who worked fulltime in the management of schools. Elementary classroom teachers taught just one grade level. In the city schools there were special classes for mentally retarded children who did not achieve the academic demands of their age and grade level. There were specialist teachers for physical education and art and music. Urban schools developed a bureaucracy, with a hierarchy of roles and specialized functions. Full-time administrators not only managed and supervised, they became the visible spokespeople for elementary and secondary education. Rural schools had few such advocates, except perhaps the county superintendents of schools (Sher, 1977; Tyack, 1974).

As America achieved world industrial predominance in the first half of the twentieth century, the techniques of factory enterprise began to take on a value of their own. Specialized factories were more efficient than the old workshops where one craftsman produced an object at a time from his own skillful hands. Automobile manufacturing was a prime example. Mass-produced automobiles were affordable. They required large factories and the breakdown of operations into steps on an assembly line. Mass production brought the workers and their families from the rural areas into "sophisticated" cities. The old-time one-room school must have seemed very backward and inefficient to the newly trained school administrators, many of whom themselves had entered teaching in order to become "professional people" (Callahan, 1962).

Influential educators, such as Ellwood P. Cubberly, began to speak openly of a general "rural problem," in which the schools were part of an endemic problem in the rural areas. In his book, *Rural Life and Education: A Study of the Rural-School Problem as a Phase of the Rural-Life Problem* (1914), Cubberly skillfully criticized many of the attributes of rural life in the early decades of the twentieth century and found it wanting in all respects. Country children were considered to be less intelligent, the teachers to be less well-prepared, and the supervision of teachers to be almost nonexistent. They were the poor county cousins of education. Ironically, the perceptions are almost reversed today, when city schools for various reasons often are seen as sites of the most difficult problems of American education.

Funded primarily by taxes on real estate, the country schools were strapped financially. Farmers were often "land rich," but "money poor." They typically raised large families, who helped on the farm and went to school when not needed on the farms. The school term generally was shorter in rural areas, in order that the farm children could help with the summer crops.

Some rural school districts closed for a week while the teachers attended teacher "institutes" in October or November so that the corn crop could be harvested with the help of the children. Even well into the twentieth century, the rural school term was completed by early May, so that the children were available for work on the farm during the busy late spring and early summer. Many farmers raised much of what they consumed and had little discretionary money to pay school taxes from cash crops.

Efficiency

The one-room schools, once built, were relatively economical to operate. Through the voluntarism of the parents, neighbors, and school directors, routine maintenance of the buildings was often accomplished with little cost to the school district. The only major expenses were in salary for a teacher, the purchase of coal and wood to heat the building, and for minimal amounts of instructional materials. Certainly when comparisons were made between the costs of urban schools and costs of rural schools, rural schools spent far less per student than urban schools during the first half of the twentieth century. But the cost per student, even in a one-room school, could be relatively high in some locations, as there were many schools with a dozen or less students enrolled, although the schools with small populations were balanced in many communities by other one-room schools that were overcrowded with forty or more students.

The location of one-room schools was a logistical problem. Ideally a school should be available within walking distance (less than two miles on passable roads) for every student. However, once the schoolhouses were built, they remained in that location for decades. Many were more than a century old when they were discontinued in the 1950s. In Richland Township, in rural Bucks County, Pennsylvania, only one of the nine one-room schools had been built in the twentieth century, and that one was completed in 1901. If the region within walking distance of a particular school had a decrease in school-age population, that individual school often had a small enrollment. On the other hand, if the local community had a great increase in school-age children, its one-room school would be overcrowded with forty students or more. As there was little, if any, public transportation available in most rural areas, it was almost impossible to equalize enrollment in the various schools in a district unless expensive school busing was utilized. School boards were innovative in dealing with overenrollments, sometimes by paying tuition for children to attend schools in neighboring school districts.

In Pennsylvania, the boundaries of the school district were ordinarily the same as that of the township. There might be four to ten separate one-room schools spread out within the township. Few of the township school districts provided any centralized services, other than the purchase and distribution of instructional materials. If they hired a special teacher in music or art, that teacher would be spending time in transit between one school and another. Until the middle of the twentieth century, when they began the process of school consolidation, most rural school districts did not have special teachers for subjects such as music, art, or physical education.

The country school teachers received very little direct or daily supervision. They were under the nominal supervision of the county superintendent of schools, who assigned an assistant superintendent to make schoolhouse observations and rate teachers. From the perspective of efficiency, these were unsatisfactory conditions. Through the 1930s, 1940s, and 1950s, Pennsylvania saw most of its rural roads paved, allowing year-round travel. Busing made school consolidation feasible, so that an entire township school district, or even two or more contiguous districts could merge resources, build a new consolidated school at a central location, and by busing the eligible students to that location, enjoy the advantages of an efficient, modern program.

Modernization and Specialization

The last point is perhaps the most important. The urban schools, with their specialization, broader curriculum, and sophisticated services, became the norms of modern education. By midcentury the one-room schools must have seemed like antiques to educational policymakers. They were, indeed, old facilities. In most cases, the buildings were not electrified until the 1930s. The outside toilets were unsanitary. Worse, they were even polluting the wells on the school property. Something had to be done to modernize the school facilities.

School consolidation was strongly advocated by policymakers. As young families were concentrating in clusters around the cities, many once-rural areas had become suburbs. They would need new schools anyway. The old rural schools would not meet any contemporary standards for school construction. The solution: Replace them with new, consolidated schools.

Another factor had an impact on the educational landscape of the late 1950s and early 1960s. This was the educational reform that was triggered by the launching of the Soviet space satellite, *Sputnik*, in 1957. In the short run this had a greater direct influence upon secondary education than upon elementary, but there was also to be a long-term ripple effect, which ensured that the face of elementary education would be changed in America. This was the movement toward larger and larger schools, for diversity of educational programs, and for efficiency of scale.

The distinguished educator and college administrator, James B. Conant, authored a report, *The American High School Today*, in 1959, which was extraordinarily influential in shaping the structure of American public education during the decades that followed. Although the target of his reform was the high school, the implications had an impact on Pennsylvania public education at the elementary level as well. One recommendation was to be the death knell for small school districts in the Keystone State.

In Conant's view, small high schools were unsatisfactory as they could not provide sufficient diversity and depth of education programs for secondary students. He recommended that high schools should be large enough to have a graduating class of at least one hundred students. The Pennsylvania legislature in 1963 required that each county superintendent of schools come up with a plan to consolidate the then existing smaller districts into large districts, which would be fully consolidated. That is, these larger districts would serve all of the public school children within them, from kindergarten to the twelfth grade. When consolidation was completed by the mid-1960s, Pennsylvania had about five hundred public school districts. Prior to school consolidation, Pennsylvania had had more than 2,500 districts providing elementary education.

The present 501 school districts vary in size, certainly. In some cases the district had to envelop an entire county to meet the standards for larger school units. A few districts, mainly in tightknit suburban communities, have maintained relatively small districts. But the norm is a kindergarten through twelfth-grade district with one thousand to fifteen thousand students, with a superintendent of schools as the chief executive officer responsible to an elected board of school directors. The superintendent manages a team of administrative and educational specialists in addition to the classroom teachers as well as a complex set of support services.

With the exception of the Amish and Old-Order Mennonites and some other religiously oriented schools, the one-room, one-teacher school is extinct as an option in the schools of Pennsylvania. Consolidated schools are now mature. Yet some would argue that they have not fulfilled all of the promises made by the advocates of school consolidation.

Criticisms of Consolidation

Perhaps the most persistent critic of the rush to school consolidation has been Jonathan P. Sher. But it was not until 1977, when Sher's revisionist book, *Education in Rural America: A Reassessment of Conventional Wisdom*, was published, that a major voice in opposition to universal school consolidation in rural areas was heard. In an essay with Stuart A. Rosenfeld therein, "The Urbanization of Rural Schools, 1840–1970," Sher and Rosenfeld provide an historical analysis of the process of school consolidation. They admit that there were benefits to school consolidation, but believe that the goal of those who were advocates of school reform "was to reshape rural schools until they became miniature replicas of America's urban (and later, suburban) schools" (Rosenfeld and Sher, 1977, 11).

Consistent with other revisionist critiques of American education of the 1960s and 1970s, Rosenfeld and Sher concentrated upon what they saw as an ideology of consolidation, which:

was an ideology of growth, efficiency and conformity designed to support the nation's rising commitment to industrialism, corporate capitalism, and urban life. It was not an ideology that rural people invented, sought, or supported. In fact, it was largely antithetical to the nature and meaning of rural life. However, this mattered little to urban reformers obsessed with saving rural children from their parents, and rural parents from themselves. This was truly a reform movement steeped in the American tradition. Just as reformers had "civilized" the Indians, and "Americanized" the immigrants, so too would they "urbanize" rural citizens through the schools. (Rosenfeld and Sher, 1977, 42)

The foregoing is too harsh a criticism of the motives and processes of rural school consolidation. Any efforts to consolidate schools based on ideology were moderated by the realities of rural life and the traditions of local governance of school districts by elected school boards. But there is certainly some truth in the assertion that the urban schools became the models of public education in the early decades of the twentieth century. However, little attention has been paid by educational historians to the ascendancy of suburban schools in the post–World War II period. Most of the school districts that emerged as a result of consolidation in the region of southeastern Pennsylvania were influenced by the processes of suburbanization more so than by an ideology based upon the values and assumptions of urban schools.

There are other contemporary critics of a total application of school consolidation. The journal of the professional educational fraternity, Phi Delta Kappa, included a featured section on rural education in the October 1995 edition of its journal, the *Phi Delta Kappan*. The lead article was by Alan J. DeYoung and Barbara Kent Lawrence. In their article, "On Hoosiers, Yankees, and Mountaineers," DeYoung and Lawrence provide a cultural and historical analysis of economic and social issues that have had an impact on rural life and education into the late twentieth century. They point out that there has been a migration of rural people into metropolitan regions, creating a dilemma about the purpose of rural schooling. The issues have been amplified because of a commitment by national and state policymakers to educational standards in order to sustain industrial predominance.

The insights of DeYoung and Lawrence into the continuity of rural life and education illuminate important issues.

Ties to community, place, and family are often strong in rural communities, and it is in the local schoolhouse where many of these attachments are formed and solidified. At the same time, the academic skills and values emphasized today often run counter to the values of place and community. This contradiction is particularly visible in places where personal relationships and attachments to place go back for generations. (DeYoung and Lawrence, 1995, 108)

In the school consolidation movement, values such as "place" and "community" were never part of the discussion. The values of the winners of the school consolidation movement were advocates of "efficiency" and "modernization." In the end, it was a contest of the objectivity of expert opinion versus the subjectivity of intrinsic values such as place and community. The education experts could amass argument and facts to support their recommendations. Rural people in general were inarticulate in the face of the experts, and thus were able to speak only softly and indistinctly in support of their little schools.

The Oral Histories

But enough time has passed so that more balanced and reflective judgments can be made about the small rural schools. This book attempts to distill some wisdom from the voices of those who attended them. Those voices will be presented in the following chapters. After audiotaping the interviews the authors then transcribed the audiotapes in full. The typed transcripts were analyzed for insights on particular topics, such as the characteristics of the teachers. Seven of the edited interviews are reported in the next chapter. These seven have been presented in approximately the chronological order in which the subjects attended or taught in one–room schools, so that historical perspective may be gained. In presenting the tales of these individuals we have eliminated our questions, so that what was a dialog reads as a coherent story. We have done some editing, eliminating some sections that, in our judgment, were not so important or were redundant. We have also corrected some grammar, but we have left some idioms that we felt conveyed the language patterns of the person interviewed.

After the individual stories we have followed a topical approach in the next two chapters, drawing from all of the interviews to gain insights on such subjects as the teacher and teaching methods, the culture of the school, games played by the students, school consolidation, and advantages and disadvantages of the one-room school experience. We conclude with some tentative lessons learned in retrospect from this study.

2

Seven Oral Histories

These interviews provide personal memories of the country-school experiences of seven individuals, covering the twentieth century to the post–World War II period.

The first individual attended several country schools in Lehigh County, near Allentown, Pennsylvania, during the first decade of the twentieth century. Interviewed when almost ninety years old the subject demonstrated the clarity of recall about her schooling that characterized most of our interviewees. She showed how important the influence of an individual teacher was, as she even moved away from her parents' home to live with an older sibling in order to be taught by a particular teacher. She provides a detailed account of the eighth-grade exam that was required of rural students in order to qualify for admission to the high school.

Our interviewee was valedictorian of all of the students in her school district. She recalled how she memorized her valedictory speech for the graduation exercises at the end of eighth grade. Three-quarters of a century after she gave it, she still remembered the response of the audience, as she received a burst of applause for her speech. She then attended high school and normal school and became a teacher in graded schools.

The second story included is that of an individual who attended a country school in Upper Bucks County a decade later, during the period of World War I and the early 1920s. He has strong recollections of his first one-room schoolteacher, who began her teaching career directly after completing high school. He also describes some events in which there was an impact of World War I upon his rural school. Like our first interviewee, he was valedictorian of the township schools. He also went on to a town high school, and he recalls his transition from the country school to the secondary school.

The third story is that of an individual who attended a country school in Bucks County during the 1920s. He also was the valedictorian of his eighth-

Students of the Rocky Ridge School, c. 1900. This photo from the archives of the Richland (One-Room School) Historical Society shows the students in the Rocky Ridge School, Richland Township. Photo reproduced courtesy of the Richland (One-Room School) Historical Society.

grade class. Although he gave us no details of his exam or the graduation ceremony, his insights are particularly useful as he details his transition to a town high school, which itself was the result of a brand-new consolidation of high schools from two small towns. Like several others whom we interviewed, he felt that there was discrimination against the country kids in the town high school. He also told of coming from a home that was Pennsylvania German in its culture while instruction in the school was in English.

The next person was also valedictorian of her grade school class. She reported that her eighth-grade teacher had held her back in the country school for a year so she and classmates would be better prepared for high school. Ironically, she never attended high school, although later in life she wrote weekly newspaper columns. Some of these columns were collected and published in books, so she became a published author without having attended high school!

She recalled the contributions of several of her teachers. One of her teachers was also her uncle. His name was Lloyd Yoder, but for two generations of students in Upper Bucks County, he was affectionately known as "Poppy" Yoder. Our informant recalls the influence that Yoder had on his students, particularly the boys. He was an outstanding role model. Later he was a high school coach and was selected by Pearl Buck to found the Welcome House for children of Asian mothers and American servicemen after World War II and the Korean War. These children would have been ostracized if they had remained in Asia after their American fathers had left following military service. Yoder and his wife adopted several Amerasian children and raised them as their own.

The fifth story is told by one of the authors of this book, who was a student in a one-room school during the later years of the Great Depression of the 1930s and during World War II. He recalled the influence of these external events upon life in the country school. Even in the relative seclusion of the countryside, the war had an effect on schooling, particularly on the values that were taught in both the formal and "hidden" curriculum.

The sixth story is that of an individual who had the unique experience of attending a country school as a student prior to World War I, then returning as a teacher to the same building about thirty-five years later. During the period between her experience as a student and then as a rural schoolteacher she graduated from high school, then from a state normal school, became a certified teacher, taught in graded urban schools, left teaching for marriage and child-rearing, then returned to her country home, became widowed, and returned to her beloved Passer School during the transitional period when school busing permitted school districts to have age-graded classes in the old country schools. In her case, the school building had two rooms, which allowed the seventh grade to be in one of the rooms and the eighth grade in the other.

During the time in which this two-room school was a de facto junior high there was a remarkable example of voluntarism in which a Parent-Teacher Association purchased a farm field of three acres and converted it into baseball diamonds and playground space. She also tells of the emotions of the students and her own strong feelings as her class of seventh-grade students left the country school to begin their studies in a brand new junior-senior high school. She compares her experiences as a teacher in the departmentalized secondary school with her fond memories of teaching seventh- and eighth-grade students in the old country school.

The last person whose story is included in this section was a young student during the transitional period of the 1950s. One of the early baby boomers, she began first grade in a country school and continued in country schools until a new consolidated elementary school was opened. She traced her subsequent academic underachievement in schooling to the fact that she had learned lessons in the earliest years by listening to the older students and resented having to relearn them later. This personal insight was in contrast with most of the other former students whom we interviewed, who regarded the opportunity to listen to other classes as they recited as an advantage.

She was also able to make comparisons between the country one-room school and the consolidated elementary school that replaced it, since the township school children were placed in a new, graded school while she was a student in the primary grades. She found the consolidated school much more formal and rule-driven than the country school.

The seven selected oral histories follow. These stories introduce themes that are explored in greater depth in later chapters.

EARLY TWENTIETH-CENTURY SCHOOL DAYS

> I added my marks and divided by nine, and I think I was more amazed than anyone else. . . . I was the best one in the whole group. . . . I was the valedictorian.
>
> —Mamie Fluck Kratzer

Mamie Fluck Kratzer attended several one-room schools in a rural area of Lehigh County near Allentown, Pennsylvania, during the first decade of the twentieth century. She also attended a four-room town school and a two-room high school. After high school she attended Kutztown Normal School (later Kutztown State Teachers College and now Kutztown University of Pennsylvania). She then became a teacher in graded schools in urban communities. At the time of this interview she was almost ninety years old. She was interviewed at her home in Allentown on November 19, 1986.

"I attended Standard School on Limeport Pike for two years. It's now used as a home. Opposite is a home where Mr. S. lived; he's the man who told me that four times six is twenty-four. Because he helped me I considered him to be my first boyfriend! My parents were Pennsylvania Dutch.

"I started first grade there in 1903. There were eight grades there, all in one room. We were not allowed to speak anything but English, although we spoke Pennsylvania Dutch at home. I suppose that I learned English just by hearing it.

The teacher spoke it and we read it in our books. The teacher said, 'You must speak it on the playground.' We did when he heard us; we didn't always speak it when he didn't hear us. We were taught English by reading and hearing others.

"The teacher taught us little songs. Did you ever play the game, 'Little Sally Waters'? That's how I learned directions. 'Point to the East, Point to the West. Point to the one that you love best.'

"There were about forty children in the school. We were always crowded. I also went to Sunday school there. People in the neighborhood ran the Sunday school. The teacher was also justice of the peace. He punished children with a stick. Hit them on the backside. I don't remember that he ever hit any of the girls. I think he felt like doing it to me, but didn't. The boys were worse, but the girls were naughty too. What I did probably was talk too much.

"The advantage of the country school was that in a one-room school the children learned a great deal from listening to others, as is still true today. Now those who aren't interested in school will probably get more help in a graded school. There couldn't be any frills or advantages like they have in schools nowadays. It was mainly reading, writing, arithmetic. That's it.

"I attended Standard School two years, then we moved to Bortz Crossing and I attended Grime's Independent School for two years. That was a one-room school. Then we moved to the town of East Texas [Pennsylvania], and I attended that school for two years. It was four rooms, two grades in each room. The teacher there was the best teacher I ever had.

"Then we moved to Laubensberger's Mill where I attended the Reigel's country one-room school for one year. The teacher was just fresh out of Kutztown [State Normal School], but she was good. At that time I already had visions of trying to pass the eighth-grade examination to qualify for admission to high school. The next year there was another young woman. I could tell by the first days of school that I would not get very far with her. Well, she was young and had all those kids. I told my dad, 'I can't learn much from her. She can't do the arithmetic problems, and we had big ones.' I said, 'Don't you think I could go back to school at East Texas if I went up there and stayed all week?' My sister lived there.

"My dad said, 'I'll ask the school directors.' It was the same district, Lower Macungie Township. They said that if the teacher is willing she may go. And the teacher was willing, so I went. That man not only taught children to learn but also, for his pride or ambition, he wanted to have the best kids in the two districts. He did often have them. He was also a music teacher. He taught me to play the organ. There was an organ in the school and we also had one at home. Now, he could inspire you to learn. He knew how.

"We trapped in class. Do you know what trapping is? He had us sit on the recitation bench; the best one sat at the head and of course all the way down. When he asked a question, if you couldn't answer it, the next one was asked and if he could answer it he went above you. And he also did that in correcting papers. We wrote our papers and the kids corrected them in class. It had to be written something like this: 'If one orange cost eight cents, what will seven oranges cost? Seven oranges will cost seven times eight cents or fifty-six cents.' I didn't realize it at that time, but he not only taught us mental arithmetic, he taught us English.

"That was the first year we had report cards. I knew that the passing mark for eighth graders was 70 percent. I prayed to make a 70 percent. I would get up at five o'clock in the morning, light the oil lamp, and do my geography. Grammar was my favorite subject; I loved diagramming. All year long my marks were in the seventies, none as high as the eighties.

"In the spring at the close of the school term, the two districts—Upper Macungie and Lower Macungie—got together and the county superintendent would come and give you a test. It was the very last of March or beginning of April that this test was held. You had to be recommended by the teacher. In our group there were four girls. One didn't want to take it but three of us took it; not any boys did in my class.

"It was held in Wescosville that year. At the examination we were admonished not to cheat. Most of the questions were written on the blackboard and we wrote the answers on paper. We had nine subjects: reading (when the superintendent had us read orally and asked questions), writing, spelling (I missed ten words out of fifty, got 80 percent), mental arithmetic, arithmetic, physiology, history, geography, and grammar.

"In the meantime, the teachers who brought their pupils had to correct the papers. Well, at the close of the day they sent us to the blackboard and assigned us a space to compute. Our scores were read in each subject. In mental arithmetic I was careless; I just skipped part of it. My others were all very good. Well, I added my marks and divided by nine, and I think I was more amazed than anyone else. My mark was ninety and five-ninths. Consequently I was the best one in the whole group of forty. Only twelve or thirteen passed. I was the valedictorian.

"If the exam were held in Lower Macungie, commencement was held in Upper Macungie, which was at the Trexlertown Church. They built a stage out over the pulpit. My teacher let me know, 'You must prepare a valedictory address and there will be one rehearsal.' But he did not offer to help. I didn't know what a 'valedictory address' was. But I wrote to my first teacher and asked if he could help me. He sent me a nicely written one for an eighth-grader. In the meantime my father asked the pastor of our church and he wrote me one which was for high school or even junior college. The woman who had taught me in seventh grade came from Kutztown to attend. She really helped me.

"I memorized that thing, and I delivered it in the church. Now, this will sound like bragging. The salutatorian was presented, somebody read an essay, and somebody played a coronet solo. You know you didn't applaud in church, but when I was through they burst out in applause. That's something I'll never forget.

"Here I was a thirteen–fourteen-year-old kid. My parents lived in the country, two and one-half miles from Emmaus and two and one-half from East Texas.

What was I to do? Well, if there were transportation I could have gone to Kutztown for high school. So the only thing I could do was go to high school in Emmaus. I walked two and one-half miles each day to get there.

"Well, I had the shock of my life going to high school in Emmaus in the Central School. Two rooms, two teachers, but the one could not maintain discipline. The kids walked around; they talked out loud. Never had I seen that before. And three or four of the subjects they had in that first year of high school were ones I had already covered. The room was so crowded, and the other teacher, who was the principal, would send you to the blackboard with a little slip of paper with maybe a problem in arithmetic or a little question in geography or history or grammar.

"Consequently I became the laziest kid in the room. Now if he had used his head he would have asked me to help the kids who didn't understand. I could have done that. I just sat there and I got the worst study habits.

"Neither of those two men teachers came back after that first year. Then there were two new men teachers. Now, they were good. But I was lazy; I didn't study more than I had to. I got along, but I wasn't valedictorian. One boy studied but I didn't. I got good marks. I graduated in three years.

"By then my parents lived in Emmaus and then they could afford to send me to Kutztown [Normal School] by taking a train. You know, tuition then was very low at Kutztown, I think only $1.75 a week, until I was seventeen and then it was only a quarter a week because when you were seventeen the state paid for it. When I was too young the school district paid for it. That paid for tuition.

"There was a train that ran once in the morning and once in the evening, Kutztown to Allentown and back. We called it the Kutztown Flyer. I went to school on that train for two years. Now listen to this. The Allentown kids had gone to high school for four years; I went three years. We were all in the same class. Those that didn't go to high school at all—like if I had gone when I graduated from eighth grade—went four years at Kutztown. A girl who had failed in the eighth-grade examination was sent directly to Kutztown and graduated a year ahead of me. Kutztown took them anyway if they were beyond eighth grade.

"We all graduated with certificates to teach in two years. Then if your teaching was satisfactory, you got your diploma. I was at Kutztown for two years and got a teaching job right after that."

Themes

A number of themes appear in this story that will be examined later in the other stories and in the analytic sections in Chapters 3 and 4. Perhaps the central theme is the importance of the teacher. Mamie Fluck Kratzer went to live with an older sister in order to be taught by a highly motivated, skilled teacher. Chapter 3 will continue our examination of the characteristics of teachers. Another theme that will reappear is the importance of the eighth-grade exam. This was a common experience in the country schools. In the case of Mamie Fluck

Kratzer the county exam and the graduation exercises were a highlight in her life. The county exam and eighth-grade graduations continued during the life of the one-room school. The insights of other individuals about the eighth-grade exams and the graduation ceremony will be presented in Chapter 3. Most of those individuals whom we interviewed also commented upon the transition to a town high school. Many had negative experiences during their first year of high school. Later in this chapter, both James Gerhart and Paul Bryan will comment upon their experiences in the town high school.

SCHOOLING DURING THE "GREAT WAR"

> I was in the eighth grade, but I was listening to the lessons in one of the lower grades. In other words, we repeated the study a little bit. But it was to our benefit. In the town school they only had one chance to learn the lessons. If they missed it, they missed it. They didn't have a chance to review like we did.
>
> —James Gerhart

James Gerhart attended a country school in Milford Township, Bucks County, during World War I. Later he attended and graduated from Quakertown High School. He was interviewed on August 30, 1986, at the Shelly School, the meeting place of the Richland One-Room School Historical Society.

"I attended the school at Brick Tavern right near East Swamp Church. I started in 1915 and went there until 1923. The school was called the Weikel School. It was founded in 1849, at the time the public schools were being started in the township. Before that, school was held in the old East Swamp Church. That was a building that was divided, part for school and part for church. There was a divider in between the school and the church that could be raised. In 1849 and 1850 the new church was built, and at that time Weikel School was started. The Weikel School was built on a small hillside there. During the time that I went, there were from thirteen to seventeen children. We were a very small school.

"My first teacher was Miss Erwinna Price from Richlandtown. My first day of school was her first day of teaching. She was not quite eighteen, I think, at the time she started teaching. She had just graduated from high school in Richlandtown. She was not old enough to get into nurse's school but she wanted to be a nurse. So she started teaching. She said, 'I never had planned to be a teacher,' but she taught for forty-three years. My other teacher was Miss Edith Weimer. She was there for my last three years at the school.

"Miss Price came from Richlandtown, about five miles away, on the trolley that was called the 'Tripper.' She changed at the Red Lion Hotel in Quakertown to the Liberty Bell trolley that went up the Old Bethlehem Pike past our school. It was Stop 97 on the trolley line from Philadelphia to Bethlehem. It would cost her not more than seven to ten cents.

"For recitation we went up front. I think most of the education we got came from listening to the other classes reciting their lessons. That is one thing that I often appreciated, listening to other grades. We already had the basis for the lesson by listening to the other grades. It was also good for a review. If you missed something, you heard the first and second graders go over it, and I think we picked it up by listening to it again.

"We never had the dunce cap for discipline. But we had to stand up on the platform in case we didn't behave ourselves. We would stand aside of [*sic*] the teacher's desk. We never had to stand in a corner. I remember I had to stand up there with one of the other fellows. I guess we were talking too much. One had to stand on one side and the other to stand on the other side of the teacher until you were a little bit tired of standing.

"The teacher never spanked anyone. But we had one family that moved in from Wilmington, Delaware, a very rough family. The father was a policeman, I think. He came when the boys didn't behave themselves in school. The teacher called his children out, and the father gave them a licking in the hall. We thought he was really getting a roughhouse there. But the teacher never hit anybody.

"We walked to school, except if it rained. Then my dad took us. We had high water then across the roads behind the school. But other than that we always walked to school.

"A good thing about the school was the closeness, the fellowship of the neighbors. Most of the neighbors were financially poor. But most of them were church people, and I think the fellowship there was very strong.

"One thing that I think that we lost out in at the school was in the singing. We had no music instruction and not much drawing either. We had penmanship training, a little bit, but not in music or in art.

"Our biggest attraction there was the blacksmith's shop that was not too far from the school. We would go over at lunch and see what the blacksmith was doing. He was hard of hearing. We offered to fetch water at the blacksmith's shop. We'd perhaps play with his fire a little bit. We sometimes pumped the bellows, and I guess sometimes we spoiled the fire for him. He'd grump a little bit, but I think he took an interest in the students. He was very friendly to us.

"In 1917–1918, during the war, the pike there was the main highway between Allentown and Philadelphia. When the army went by in the big trucks, the school was dismissed and we would go out. Perhaps the teacher was more interested in seeing the soldiers, and she would be attracted, perhaps more so than we were. But we stood outside to watch the whole caravans going past. The American war trucks always traveled seven trucks together. When they went past it was quite a thing. It was chain-drive Macks that they had. They made a lot of noise.

"The schoolhouse was used for selling war savings bonds. All the neighbors came in. I was quite small. Henry Hallman, the iceman, was the man who had charge of selling the war savings bonds. I remember one little story that he told about a man doing some selling. A billy goat came along and bumped him in the back and he said, 'Good help. Give me another boost like that.' And that's what he felt that we ought to have there to buy bonds.

"We had to go to Milford Square to take the eighth-grade examination. That was in 1923, and all the schools from the township came together. I think it was nine or eleven schools. At that time they didn't want too many country children to come to Quakertown High School, so the examination was quite hard, because if the students didn't pass they couldn't go to high school. There were only seventeen that passed, out of over forty that took the test.

"I've often felt that I could have taken the examination for high school a year before, but it would not have been to my benefit, because I was listening to the lessons in the other grades during that last year. I was in the eighth-grade class, but I was listening to the lessons in one of the lower grades. In other words, we repeated the study a little bit. But it was to our benefit. In the town school they only had one chance to learn the lessons. If they missed it, they missed it. They didn't have a chance to review like we did.

"We had a township graduation at Sheetz's Lutheran Church, at Spinner-stown. That was in 1923. The church was filled. We had a prayer. Reverend Lutz from Pennsburg was the speaker. He was quite a prominent speaker. I was vale-dictorian, and I had to make a speech. The teacher did most of the writing. I give her most of the credit for it. She typed it out. 'Climb, though the Rocks Be Rugged' is the name of the thing.

"Then I went to Quakertown High School. We went by trolley. We had to do some of the farm work in the morning before I went to school. I often wondered afterward if we got cleaned up adequately. Before school I fed the pigs. Then we went with the trolley. I'd try to get the ten-after-three trolley to go home, because it gave me more time in the afternoon to work. I was supposed to get home right after school. I never went out for sports at the high school because our exercise wasn't in sports, but working the farm.

"It was a big change to go to high school, especially in art. I was supposed to take art, and that was one of my hardest problems in school. I couldn't even draw a picture. Music was the same way. That was the hardest thing for the country kids—the subjects that we didn't have any training in. Or in sports, either, because we had no training in baseball or football. I had no problems in marks in regular classes, but in art and music we were altogether out.

"We felt like we were outsiders in high school. The best friend that we had was the science teacher, Miss Weinberger. She herself had come from our township, and she knew the families. She was the best encouragement we ever had."

Themes

The importance of repetition was again described in this story. Even the eighth-graders would benefit from listening to the lower grades as they recited. The methodology of teachers will be analyzed further in Chapter 3. The country

students were handicapped when they went to high school as there were performance skill areas, such as art, music, and organized sports in which they had no
training. The transition to high school is described in the next story and discussed more fully in Chapter 4. The farm children were expected to help with the
chores before and after school, which meant that they had few opportunities for
extra-curricular activities in the high school. Paul Bryan, in the next interview,
came from a very large farm, which restricted his after-school activities as well.

The importance of the network of trolleys in the early part of the century,
when most families could not afford an auto, was a factor in providing a means
for both teachers and students to travel to and from school, as is illustrated in
this story.

A FARM BOY GOES TO SCHOOL IN BUCKS COUNTY

Being a shy country boy, you knew that you were looked down at.
They sort of felt that a farm boy was not up to their classification.
—Paul Bryan

Paul Bryan was a student in a one-room school in East Rockhill Township
during the 1920s. He was valedictorian of his township, then went on to high
school. He then attended Michigan State University as a student in agriculture.
He returned to Bucks County as an agricultural extension agent and as a dairy
farmer. He was interviewed at his farm in Bedminster Township on July 25,
1987.

"When I went to the Steeley School during the 1920s, I was number five of
eight children. I had three different teachers. Their names were Miss Canna, Mrs.
Bertha Fretz, and Mr. William Youngkin. They were all good teachers, but I
particularly recall Mrs. Bertha Fretz. She was kind and considerate, and she
wanted her students to do well in school. She drove you in reading, writing, and
arithmetic.

"There were approximately thirty to thirty-five students in the eight grades.
Sometimes there was only one student in a grade. If the student was halfway
bright the teacher usually put you in the next grade.

"One of the main advantages of the one-room school was that you were
close to home. No busing was needed. You got to interact with older children,
and visa versa with the younger ones. As a younger student, you listened and
observed older grade material. Really, it was progressive learning at your own
speed. Younger and older children played together at recess and dinnertime. You
always chose up sides for games so everybody got to participate.

"Now, some of the main disadvantages of the one-room school: You had no
athletic competition among other schools. You had very little library material.
The music was very limited. You only sang songs at the morning exercises.

"A small amount of land around the school was used for a playground. We
had a porch on the school and underneath the porch to one side was a coal bin

that we used for storage. Inside the school, you had a front platform with the chalkboards along the back of the front platform. The teacher's desk was on the platform. On one small corner of the platform was a small bookcase. That was the extent of our library. A big potbellied stove was in the back of the room, surrounded by shelves to hold your lunches. Clothes racks were in the rear, on both sides of the building. We had six or seven rows of school desks, with class seats in front of the rows of desks, facing the blackboard. You had a hallway coming in from the outside of the school for the entrance. In this hallway also was a rope, coming down from the bell. The rope was pulled to ring the school bell. Bigger students or the teacher rang the bell. It was a privilege.

"We didn't have electricity. We only had school during the day, so we didn't need electricity. I remember at that time, too, on the farms we just used lanterns for our light. At the school we had two outside toilets, one for the males, one for the females. The drinking water came from a dug well on the school ground. When you wanted to drink, although you had cups, what you usually did was put your hands under the spout and pump slowly and then put you mouth down to your hand and drink.

"The heating system was one big potbellied stove. In really cold weather the kids put on their coats and sat next to the stove to keep warm. The teachers would come a little early in the morning on Monday and use wood to start the fire. Usually the coal was fixed in the stove to hold over until the next day. The teacher did most of that.

"We all helped with chores. Once a week we participated in washing the chalkboards. Some privileged students got the honor of going out with the erasers and clapping them outside so the dust would go into the air. The floors were mopped on Friday afternoon, so it was clean for the weekend and the beginning of the next week. I remember that occasionally one of the students would walk about a half-mile to the school board treasurer's home for the teacher's paycheck. That was a privilege.

"We lived a mile from the school and walked to school. Occasionally, Dad took us to school by horse and sled during the snowy season. School was closed during the big storms. At that time no highway workers opened the roads. Just the horse and the buggy and the sleds opened the way. If the roads had too much snow on them you drove and walked through the fields where the snow wasn't so deep. If the roads weren't open we knew there was no school. And, I remember that our teacher had a Model-T Ford, and he came by our farm. We kept our eye open in snowy weather, to see when that Model-T Ford went by.

"All of us walked to school. We chatted with other students around the outside toilet. Why there? Well, we tried to keep out of the view of the teacher so he wouldn't know who was there, because if he saw you, he got you to come in and write a song on the board for our morning exercises, and none of us went for that, so we sort of hid until the bell rang to come in for school. At recess and lunchtime we played games. After school we walked home and helped to do dairy barn chores. We milked the cows by hand.

"We had an hour lunch period. The students all carried their lunch and we sat at our desks and ate it, but we ate it lickety split so we could go outside and play. We played baseball. There wasn't room to play real baseball, but we made our ground rules according to the amount of land we had. There was a farmer's field next door. We knew to stay out of his crops.

"I remember when a new student couldn't understand or talk the English language. He knew German. We had Pennsylvania Dutch from our home. So the teacher had me sit with him on one student seat and give him instruction in the Pennsylvania Dutch language. I would interpret for him.

"One of my happiest and proudest moments was when we had final tests for graduation from the eighth grade in the township. We went to one school and all the eighth-graders got together and took these tests. I guess what made me happy was that I ended up being valedictorian of the township.

"After eight years in the Steeley School I attended high school. I used my bike to go to school, which was about a mile and a half from our home. At that time it was called Sell-Perk High School. We were the first freshman class there in 1930. There were no buses. Since I came from the surrounding township the township had to pay the tuition for the students that either came by bikes or by car. The school was built right on the borough lines of Sellersville and Perkasie.

"The high school building was new. The outside of the building was finished, and most of the equipment was there for the classrooms. When we used to have our meetings with the high school principal in the morning before our classes, we'd stand around the stage in the auditorium, because the seats hadn't been put in the auditorium at that time. The seats were there but they weren't installed. The same way in the classrooms. The seats were there but they had to install them at the proper place.

"We had academic courses, general, and commercial. I was in the academic. When we moved from the one-room school to high school, all the town kids were in section 9A in the academic course I'm talking about. All country kids were in 9B. Being a shy country boy, you knew that you were looked down at. They sort of felt that a farm boy was not up to their classification.

"But what makes me angry? You know, you didn't talk Pennsylvania Dutch, because you were sort of ashamed of it. But now in later life, it's exactly turned around. The town people want to be country people, and they want to learn Pennsylvania Dutch. You just took it that you were not quite as good as the town kids. But then as time went on, and by the time you graduated, that feeling all disappeared, we were one. It helped that we were all in the same groups in the sophomore, junior, and senior years.

"We had good teachers, and you went to Latin class, or English class, or algebra class, and you did your best, whether you felt you were from the country or not. I remember being in the country school you never heard the words 'algebra' or 'Latin.' It wasn't until you got to high school, where you were put in Latin and algebra classes, which was all Greek to me. I remember appreciating Latin, how that helped you with your English language, definitions of words, and things like that. I also remember algebra. I remember the first marking period. I got a B. All of a sudden I caught on, and the rest of the time I got As.

"In 1930 we were the first freshman class entering Sell-Perk High School, and the athletic field was just a number of loads of dirt, which trucks dumped on the field. At noontime, after we ate our lunch, the sophomores would take the freshmen out on the field to pick stones. By 1934, when we graduated, the athletic field was good enough to play football games on, and the baseball diamond and the track were ready for use. I wanted to play sports, but I was small for my age.

"What really kept me back from athletics was about one hundred head of cattle at home. We had to come home right after school to milk the cattle by hand. Before we went to school you got up at five o'clock and did chores, ate your breakfast, quick cleaned up, and got on your bike, and hoped the bicycle chain wouldn't break until you got to school. More than once my chain would break, and you and the bike raced to school to get there in time.

"We bought our present farm in 1945, and at that time I was on the Bedminster Township School Board, where we had one-room schools. The next step in consolidation was the addition of buses in our township. Kids still went to one-room schools, but only one or two grades to a school. Then the next step was the formation of the Deep Run Valley School District, with overseeing by the supervisor, Margaret Seylar. I was a school board director, and at the time Hilltown Township also had a high school. So for a number of years we had the Deep Run Valley School District. Then, it was just a natural progression to keep growing and the townships couldn't take care of the high school thing so it was a natural thing for the Pennridge district to develop, which took in Sellersville, Perkasie, and four or five townships, which is the present set-up."

Themes

In those preelectricity days, a dairy farm required hand labor for the many chores on the farm. That was a first priority, as James Gerhart had explained, and the same was true for Paul Bryan. The transition to high school was difficult for country scholars, even those as well motivated as Paul Bryan and James Gerhart. The use of Pennsylvania German was a double-edged sword. In the "sophisticated" environment of the high school, one was ashamed of a Dutch accent, but Paul Bryan's knowledge of Pennsylvania Dutch allowed him to help a German boy to become successful in the country school. An analysis of the influence of the Pennsylvania German culture is provided in Chapter 4.

TEACHERS REMEMBERED

> I think that those teachers must have been super people. They
> taught every subject, every grade. . . . They really did a job. The
> teachers were extremely dedicated.
>
> —Ruth Hackman

Ruth Hackman was a student in country schools in East Rockhill and Hill-town Townships, in Bucks County. One of the schools she attended was the Steeley School, the same school Paul Bryan attended. She and her husband later became proprietors of Hackman's Book Store in Allentown. For years Mrs. Hackman wrote a weekly column that was published in the Allentown *Morning Call* newspaper. Later many of these folksy articles were collected and published in two books.

"I went to school right across the road from the present Pennridge High School. It was a one-room school called Steeley's School. I went there from sixth through eighth grades. Prior to that I went to the Hunsberger School on the road between Dublin and Blooming Glen, in Hilltown Township, until I was in the fourth grade. Then I went one year to the Blooming Glen School. Then we moved up to East Rockhill Township, where I finished sixth through eighth grade at Steeley's School.

"My uncle was my teacher when I was in fifth grade at the Blooming Glen School. The stadium for the Pennridge School District is named Poppy Yoder Stadium. That's my uncle. He was very well respected. He was kind but fair. He just demanded respect. During the one year that I went there, though I was his niece there was no favoritism. His own daughter was also in the school. We had cousins who went to that school, also.

"Earlier I had had a real good first- and second-grade teacher in 1929–31, as well. I had her for two years. Her name was Mrs. Keeler. Then I had another teacher for third and fourth and then of course my uncle. When we moved up to Steeley, I had two sisters there as teachers. The first one I had was Ildah Fluck and then later on I had her sister, Elsie Miller.

"Even though I was valedictorian when I graduated eighth grade, I didn't go to high school. The three highest in the township's graduating classes were all from my one-room school. Maybe twenty or so graduated from the eighth grade in the whole township. Of that group, there could be maybe six who went on to high school.

"The teacher from my eighth grade is still living. In fact, her daughter wrote me about a book that I had written. I was thrilled to autograph it for her, because I was lousy in English, especially correct usage. But a lot of those things come with work. I've written two books. I just wrote one that came out last year. In '67 I wrote one and one last year.

"If you read, you get self-educated. I feel that I got a well-rounded education in the one-room school. I remember we used to have literary societies on a Friday afternoon. We had debates. They would call the meeting to order just like Roberts' Rules of Order and they were just little kids. They would have debates or perhaps a program. There were plays, and they were funny plays.

"There was a stage, which was just a platform where the teacher's desk was. The platform was maybe six or eight inches higher than the main floor. The benches for when you went up to class were at the edges of the platform. When the teacher called the students up to class, we went up to the benches near the teacher to have our class. Our library, which was usually a single bookcase, was on the platform. Sometimes they had one bookcase on each end of the platform, which was all across the front. The blackboards went along the front of the room. The stove was in the back of the room and that was tended by the teacher. She had to come over the weekend and take care of that stove, or somebody from the neighborhood had to do it. Only one of the schools that I went to, the one at Steeley's, had a water pump. In the other schools the students carried the water from a neighbor's well. They would take a stick about a yard long. It had a notch in it and they would take a bucket and go to a neighbor at Hunsberger's School. In Blooming Glen School they had a stone jug in the school, where you got your drinks. The jug was some sort of ceramic, like pickle crocks. It had a little faucet at the bottom. I think that everybody drank out of the same cup. I'm sure that the water wasn't too cold after a while.

"My eighth-grade teacher, Mrs. Fluck, thought that you got to high school too young. So she would keep you back in seventh or eighth grade for the second year, so you were more ready to go to high school. There were quite a few of us that did that. I don't know how she got away with it. It really didn't matter for me, because I didn't go to high school anyway.

"In that school, we had no special classes. We had two boys, two brothers, in our school. The one was thirteen and still in first grade. I don't know how old his brother was but the child was big. He was a big tall boy, and he was still in first grade. I remember his coming to school and he still wasn't really trained right. I remember him being out on the playground. He never could get into the games, because he wasn't intelligent. But he would cheer. I often thought about them. I don't know if it did him a disservice, or helped the others to accept people like that. He just eventually got old enough to quit school.

"At that time, if children were real bright, they skipped grades. At Blooming Glen School we had some students who skipped grades. They were real smart; they could listen to everybody else in the school, so in a sense you could get the next grade's education.

"I think that those teachers must have been super people. They taught every subject, every grade, and they were in the room with you. The classroom was the only place where they could go. They had to tend the fire, and they came weekends, sometimes, unless a neighbor would tend the fire to keep it going. They really did a job. The teachers were extremely dedicated, to be able to get into all those subjects and to do a good job and to keep twenty-eight kids organized.

They had to keep the others occupied while some of the students were up in the front of the class reciting.

"We had to learn to concentrate, and do your own work, at your desk, while all that was going on. I learned to concentrate. I remember being able to sit in a room at home and read a book when everybody was talking.

"While we didn't have any art or music like they have now, we did sing every morning. We had a piano. We had the *Golden Book of Favorite Songs.* Usually one of the pupils played. We had history and geography, and English and spelling, of course. Penmanship was a big subject. We had one of those penmanship books; we had the Palmer Method. We had to make circles, then swing around. I remember that Mrs. Fluck had a sister who taught in the Coal Regions [of northeastern Pennsylvania] and Mrs. Fluck would bring papers in of things that they made using circles and strokes, beautiful pictures, with flowers, and a basket part which was just beautiful.

"Repetition was an advantage. You see, if you hear that Harrisburg is the capital of Pennsylvania one time you might not remember, but then if you hear it a couple of times from the other classes eventually you know it because it's been reinforced.

"My favorite teacher was Mrs. Miller, but not because she was a great teacher. Her sister was a much better teacher, as far as seeing that it all got done. But Mrs. Miller was a mother teacher. You know, there's a difference in teachers. I just think of her as a very favorite teacher. Maybe it was because she was my last one. I also had a good teacher in the first grade, too, and that's very important. I think the first grade is so important because all your basics are learned there. Well, now it's almost in kindergarten when you learn your basics, because learning your letters has been put back to kindergarten. Kindergarten now is almost like first grade used to be. During the first grade you're laying the groundwork for spelling and for reading.

"I get sick of hearing people say, 'Oh, what will I ever need this subject for?,' because you don't know what you're going to need. Anything that can enlarge your vision, even to talking right, to talk sensibly, is a help. Sometimes I think they just neglect some of those important subjects. I wish I had Latin, to get to the root words. Without it I'm limited. I would like it for English. But it's a thing of the past.

"For opening exercises we always had prayer and reading the Bible. There was controversy about saluting the flag where my husband was raised, over in Souderton, only about seven miles away. In our area, I don't remember a question of saluting the flag, whether we should or not. The only people who did object were the Jehovah's Witnesses. But for the Mennonite people that was a big question. Should you or shouldn't you? Yet, many parents were Mennonites and they never questioned that. In my region, only the Jehovah's Witnesses wouldn't do it.

"The younger students sat up front. Some of the fellows seemed awful big. If you would put first-graders in the same school today with eighth-graders people would object. The older children probably picked on the younger ones. They were kids just like they are today. I remember one fellow; he was such a tease. He knew he could upset me, so on the way up to recite he would quick get into my double desk seat with me. Then he'd go on. It just bothered me so.

"Outside after lunch or recess the students played ball. They kicked the wicket, and played a lot of hopscotch, and 'Tickeley Over.' For hopscotch, they'd make the lines in the ground with a stick. After a month or so, these would look like little ditches.

"We had a coal bin right out on the porch. That's where the boys would get the coal. The girls would wash the blackboard, clap the erasers, and clean the floors. Every so often the district would come through and oil the floor so it wouldn't be dusty. What a mess that would be! I wore long stockings. Oil would be over your stockings.

"The children would have to sweep or dust. We washed the blackboard, and we'd go out and clap the erasers outside. Of course, you'd ring the bell. The bell rang for 'books,' when it was time for class to start. When the bell would ring you'd say, 'books'; in other words, school would start. When the bell would ring it was time to go into the schoolhouse in the morning. The teacher rang it at night to close school. A rope hung down into the room. Sometimes the naughty boys or naughty girls would ring it for mischief.

"Everybody called my uncle 'Poppy.' From the time he was a little boy, he was called Poppy. There was a group that was working on the roads. We had a quarry; the quarry had a crusher on the side of the road near our house. There was an old Italian man who worked on this road, and his name was Poppy, and he was a really good friend of Uncle Lloyd. Then they started to call Uncle Lloyd, 'Poppy,' too, and that name stuck with him. It transferred from this Italian fellow who was working on the road. He kind of befriended the little boy.

"My uncle used to get boys that they couldn't handle at other schools. They'd send them to him. I remember he had one guy who was sent there, and my uncle said something about they'd get to know each other, and this guy said 'Oh, yeah,' or something like that, and my uncle said, 'We may get to know each other very soon,' and he would shake the boy. But you know those boys respected him. Oh, they were just his best friends. He never had to whip them. He shook them if they were disrespectful. He would not take that talk. He was very fair. He was the ultimate of fairness. He didn't hold it against them.

"When he died, he was buried over at Sellersville. There were a couple of really tough boys who came to the funeral. He had been working with them that year, and they just stood there and stood there at his grave. He died while he was still teaching. He had a heart attack.

"He and his wife had Pearl Buck's first Welcome House. The Welcome House was where they'd bring the Asian children. In fact, he lived in Pearl Buck's house. That's how it was started. They lived there until he died in a house she owned, not her own home. They must have raised about eight or nine Asian children, besides their own. He went to a game, where his stepson David was playing, out in Lancaster, and Uncle Lloyd died at that game, and his son David never knew until the game was over.

"I walked to school. Walking, of course, was the standard thing in the lower grades. But then when I got up to Steeley's School, there were some children transported by bus. They would have lived too far away to walk. That was the beginning of consolidation. I had about a mile to walk to all three schools. There were times that I was taken to school. But on most days, we walked. Some of us would walk together. When I went to Hunsberger School I walked through the woods half of the way by myself. Sometimes the milk truck would pick me up. He would pick up the milk at the farm, and he would pick me up as I walked to school. I distinctly remember once my grandfather didn't want to take me. I wanted him to take me, and then it started to rain, so pretty soon he came after me, and took me to school. I got him to feel sorry for me.

"I think that I always enjoyed school. You know, some kids hated it. I got a C in deportment one time. My mother refused to sign that report card. I was so upset, and so worried, but she would not sign that report. Finally she did. I'll tell you, that was my last C. I never got a C again."

Themes

In this story we have a rich description of the schoolroom and of the school program. The children were expected to help with chores. This theme and others related to the culture of the school will be developed in Chapter 4. Mrs. Hackman described the strategies that teachers used in dealing with children of differing abilities. Her teachers responded to mental retardation by retaining a student in the first grade, even though he was thirteen years of age. Conversely, the bright students were accelerated *through* the curriculum. This was justified as the students could listen to other classes reciting. This repetition was seen as an advantage by many people. One teacher even retained students in the upper grades so that they would be better prepared for high school. Ironically, although Ruth Hackman was the highest ranking student in her graduating eighth-grade class, she did not go to high school. The last paragraph refers to a grade in deportment, or behavior. Students received a grade in deportment, just as they did in the academic subjects.

CULTURE, VALUES, AND WORLD WAR II

It was patriotic to collect scrap materials to be converted into military use. Miss Mae sent us out one nice spring afternoon on a mission to find scrap materials and to bring them back to the school.

—Robert Leight

Robert Leight was a student in a one-room school from 1938–46, during the Great Depression and World War II. This story was written as a memoir, rather than obtained through an interview.

"I entered Scholl's School, in Richland Township, Bucks County, in September 1938. Scholl's School was located on a winding unpaved road. The school was about a mile and one-quarter from our home. The schoolhouse was old, having been built in 1867. The exterior was plastered an off-white. Probably the building was native stone underneath. The school lot was no more than a half-acre. On one edge of the lot was a wooden coal and wood bin. Two outside toilets were the only other outbuildings. A barbed wire fence separated the school yard from the neighbor's pasture. There was a small stream close to the fence on one side. A wooden bridge crossed the creek, which was generally dry when we came back to school in the late summer, but would flood the school yard when there were melting snow and heavy rains in the late winter or early spring.

"The schoolhouse was one large room. There were three windows each on two sides. The lights on the ceiling were almost new in 1938, as the electric lines had been run along the roadway only a few years earlier. Heat was provided by a coal and wood stove which was in one of the back corners. In the other corner were shelves for our lunches and hooks for our coats. School desks were screwed to the wooden floor. They were arranged so the smaller desks were in the front. Open seats were on the front desks, close to a raised platform where the teacher's desk was located. The American flag still had forty-eight stars and it hung to the left of the teacher's desk. An unfinished portrait of George Washington hung on the wall behind the teacher's desk.

"Our teacher had just completed her certification at Kutztown State Teachers College. She had us call her Miss Mae, which was a blessing as we had to print her name on all of our papers, and Miss Mae was easier to print than Miss Rosenberger. She was very youthful and very pretty. When I showed her school picture to my mother's unmarried brothers, they joked that they were going to come back to school. Perhaps she was too modern for some of the families, as I learned as I walked home with two sisters. They remarked that it was a topic of conversation in their home that teacher wore lipstick and nail polish!

"At first my mother brought me to school. No one else came to school from the entire one-mile stretch of Tollgate Road until I was in the third grade, when my sister Dorothea was almost six and entered the first grade. My brother Richard started school two years later. Thus, for four years, from my fifth grade until the end of grade eight, there were three Leight siblings in the school. There were a number of other families with multiple students as well.

"The teacher had a bell which she kept on her desk, and at 8:45 a.m. she came to the porch and rang the bell. Opening exercises included a reading by the teacher or an older student of ten verses from the Bible, recitation of the Lord's Prayer, and the Pledge to the Flag, followed by singing of favorite songs. When the schoolhouse was cold in the morning we did calisthenics to warm up.

"The lessons began when the first grade was called to the front seats to begin their recitation in reading. When they had completed their lesson, they were given an assignment of seat work and the second-graders began their recitation. Each grade completed its lessons in a particular subject field. Older students sat farther back in larger seats, and they would often remain in their seats as the teacher conducted discussion with the class that was reciting. For math, all grade levels could be called to the blackboard to work problems on the board. The teacher conducted perhaps thirty or forty classes a day. Although the teacher was engaged with a particular class almost continually the schedule provided time for individual students to work at their own pace on the assigned seat work. Students who could complete their work rapidly would have time to draw or read or daydream, or to tune in or out on the dialog between the teacher and the other classes. I did all of those.

"In mid-morning there was a recess of fifteen minutes. In good weather, students were expected to go outside. Noon brought an hour-long lunch period, as some of the students who lived close to the school went home for a hot lunch. I never did. My mother would pack a lunch kettle, which I kept on a shelf in the back of the room. There was time to play after we had eaten our lunch. At one o'clock the schoolwork resumed. The afternoon session was divided by another recess of fifteen minutes. About ten minutes were allotted to cleaning up before dismissal at 3:45. Older students swept the wooden floor while other students were assigned to clap the erasers, wash the blackboard, bring in wood or coal, or other jobs.

"Miss Mae was the teacher for most of the first five years that I went to Scholl's School, although she married and took two leaves of absence while she was starting her own family. Then we had short-term substitutes. During my last three years Mrs. Esther Kurtz was the teacher. She had taught my older brother and sister about a dozen years previously, while she was still Miss Esther Neidig. After she had married and raised her two children to school age she returned to Scholl's School to replace Miss Mae [now Mrs. Trumbauer] when Mrs. Trumbauer decided to stay home with her own children.

"My two teachers were contrasts in personality. Miss Mae was youthful and outgoing, while Mrs. Kurtz was more reserved. Mrs. Kurtz was perhaps closer to the stereotype of a typical schoolmarm. I don't remember either teacher ever striking a child. I do have a vivid memory of one of the substitutes, feeling that she needed to prove that she was in charge, using a stick to whip an older boy until he cried in front of the entire school. But the two regular teachers maintained discipline in more humane ways.

"About the fifth grade, a boy about my age entered school. As he was behind in his academic skills he was placed one grade behind his age peers. He lived in the backwoods with his mother and a younger brother. His hair was long and his clothing was rougher than the rest of us, who had school clothing. He was the boy who was publicly whipped by the substitute teacher. We didn't know that he had a brother until the youngster was brought to school with his mother by a well-dressed woman, probably a social worker or a truant officer. He was eight years old and had never attended school. Because of compulsory education laws he had to come to school. But he was so upset that he ran off and hid behind a tree. His mother tried to persuade him to come in but he was as frightened as a wild animal. He ran off several times, but eventually he came to school regularly and fitted into the school routines.

"One of the first tasks was to learn manuscript printing, which was called penmanship. Printing led to cursive writing which was taught by the Palmer Method. The Palmer Method used an elaborate system of strokes and circles, which were expected to provide a warm-up to cursive writing. We certainly had an excellent foundation in basic arithmetic, learning the multiplication tables by memorization and mastering decimals and fractions. We had math problems in computing interest and calculated the areas of circles and other geometric figures.

"Geography was an important subject, which we studied every year from the third grade on. In the eighth grade we studied the regions of the United States and memorized the capitals of the forty-eight states. Alaska and Hawaii were still territories.

"I developed a strong interest in history. In the early grades we studied great men and women from history, keyed to the months. For instance, we studied about Columbus in October.

"We were provided a systematic background in grammar and spelling. Spelling was taught from a list of six new spelling words a day, Monday through Thursday, with a test over all twenty-four words on Friday. We had to write the words we missed at least twenty times each. Spelling and math would also be used for competitions, as we had spelling and math 'bees.' The spelling bees were often held on Friday afternoons, when we would have lighter activities, such as recitation of poetry and singing.

"I feel that I received a good foundation in the basics. My family, particularly my mother, took a strong interest in my schoolwork and helped with homework.

"Especially during the war, we were expected to conserve. For example, the furnace did not burn the coal completely, so one task for both boys and girls was to pick through the ashes after they had cooled and been thrown outside, to find lumps of coal that could still be burned. We were also expected to conserve paper, as it was scarce during the war.

"It was taken for granted that the school would exhibit Christian values. Patriotism and religion were exhibited in the opening exercises, as the recitation of the Lord's Prayer was followed by the Pledge to the Flag. Both patriotism and religion were reinforced by the singing of religious and patriotic songs.

"We played games such as baseball, 'Giggely Over,' and 'Prisoner's Base.' 'Giggely Over' was a game in which a ball was thrown over the schoolhouse to another team. [The game is explained more fully in Chapter 4.] The coal bin and the outside toilets were good places to hide when we played hide and seek. The name of one game was influenced by the big war in Europe and Asia. This game was called 'War' and was a group adaptation of 'Prisoner's Base.' There were two teams. For one team the base was the pump stand; the other team used a porch post as the base. Members of teams would run out and try to avoid being tagged by someone from the other team who had left the base more recently. In this game the members of a team could stretch the base by holding hands. One was still considered to be on base if he or she was anchored by a human chain to one of the bases.

"In both 'War' and 'Giggely Over' those students who were captured continued playing, but on the team which had captured them. The flexibility of these invented games stimulated creativity, and they were a healthy mix of cooperation and competition.

"Even conventional games had to be modified to the school conditions. By my seventh grade, someone brought a real football and we crawled under the barbed-wire fence to the pasture to play an adaptation of football. The rules were simple. As I was by then one of the bigger boys, I was to take the ball and bull ahead as far as I could until the smaller kids on the other team could pull me down. After I was stopped and pulled down, the other team was given its chance. I don't remember anyone being hurt, but we did have to be careful to avoid fresh cow manure on the pasture playing field.

"A more dangerous activity was to play on the ice when the creek froze over. Most us did not have skates but some had sleds. Those with sleds would get a running start to the edge and 'belly flop' onto the creek. Those without sleds could get a running start and slide as far as they could on their feet on the ice. The creek became dangerous when the ice began to melt, and we broke through the rotting ice. If you slipped through and got a wet foot, this was called a 'wettie.' Other things could go wrong on the ice. Once a boy wrestled me down. I came down headfirst and came up with a mouthful of ice and a loose front tooth. Even though I was in pain I never told the teacher or my parents, as I felt that it would get me and the other boy in trouble. The nerve in the tooth died and over many years the tooth became discolored. About forty years after the accident, I had root canal work and had the tooth bleached.

"One lunch hour when the ice was strong many of the older students decided to explore as far as we could go on the frozen creek. We went so far that we didn't hear the one o'clock bell and returned to the school very late. As almost all of the students were tardy, we received no punishment other than a good lecture.

"In inclement weather we could amuse ourselves inside with conventional games such as checkers and bingo. Paper was scarce, but games such as tic-tac-toe or hangman could be played on the blackboard. At other times the teacher might organize the entire school for indoor group games, such as musical chairs.

"One of the benefits of the instructional patterns of the one-room school was the amount of time that I had for reading. I learned to budget my time so that my assigned work got done on time, but I still found considerable time for recreational reading. I can still remember the first time that I read a book independently. Miss Mae had set up a table with books for browsing. I finished my assignments, sat down at the table, and found a story. It was about an American Indian boy who won a contest threshing wild rice. The plot was simple, but the fact that I could read it myself whetted my interest in both reading and history.

"Our lending library was a single bookcase. Compared to the assortment of books that are available in any elementary school today, the contents of that bookcase would seem paltry, but to me it was a gold mine. It was very eclectic, containing a range of publications which included an outdated *Philadelphia Evening Bulletin Almanac*, but it also had classics such as *Moby-Dick*. *Moby-Dick*, *The Last of the Mohicans*, *Penrod*, and *The Call of the Wild* were my favorites. I read all of the books of fiction at least once, and books such as *The Call of the Wild* several times. There was then no community lending library, so that small bookcase and its contents were about the only source of books that I had outside of our home.

"Miss Mae was very active in promoting evening programs which were called PTAs. I believe that we had an evening meeting once per month during the years in which she taught. In these programs we sang, put on short plays, and recited poetry in front of an audience of parents and friends. We strung a curtain on a wire and the teacher's platform became a stage.

"My brother and sister had joined me in school by the fifth grade. By that time there were other younger children of neighbors who lived along the way who came to school with us. By the time that I was eleven or twelve there were about five of us who took the homeward trek. In good weather we took our time. We discovered that there were four-leaf clovers growing in the grass along the side of the road and began to try to collect them. We took our treasures home and pressed them in books. We often took a leisurely forty-five minutes to walk the mile and a quarter from school to home.

"On December 7, 1941, the United States became involved in World War II. The war affected us even in our isolated school. Gasoline was rationed, so we walked to and from school more often. Paper was scarce, but this did not provide relief from writing the spelling words that we missed. As a means of conserving paper we wrote our misspelled words on the horizontal lines, then turned the paper on its side and wrote between the lines. We were told that people did this long ago when postage was very expensive. Once I studied the wrong word list and missed five of the six words. I had to write each of the five misspelled words five columns each or more than six hundred words. My plea that we needed to save paper had no effect on Mrs. Kurtz.

"It was considered to be patriotic to collect scrap materials to be converted into military use. Miss Mae sent us out one nice spring afternoon. Our mission was to find scrap materials and bring them back to the school. My sister and I and a few other students set off in the opposite direction from our home. We scavenged through junk piles along the road without much success. We thought that we had a real find when a man gave us an old automobile tire, as tires were rationed. My sister and I took turns rolling the heavy tire along the dirt road while our friends dropped off at their homes. We had no watches. When we got back to school the sun was low in the western sky and the school door was locked. Miss Mae had gone home. We also headed home. We knew it was late so we asked the farmer's wife who lived at the intersection of the dirt road and Toll-gate Road if we could take a shortcut through the farmer's clover field. She said that we could, but just this once. This shortcut saved us perhaps a quarter mile. Although we hurried, we were at least an hour late when we arrived home, to the relief of our worried mother. Later we found that the tire was too rotted to be of any use.

"In order to help to fund the war effort, students could purchase war stamps for ten cents each. When you had 187 stamps, you added a nickel, and turned them in for a war bond priced at $18.75. At maturation, in ten years, these war bonds would be valued at $25.00. Given the very low interest rates of the Depression, this seemed to be an excellent return.

"Like other schools during the war, we conducted fire and air raid drills. Students practiced sitting under their desks for protection from potential bombing raids. As there was only a single entrance to the school. Mrs. Kurtz developed a strategy for evacuation in case that door was obstructed. The windows were about four feet from the ground, so the older boys were assigned to jump out first and catch the younger students as they dropped from the window sill.

"Beside the radios and newspaper in our homes, we followed the progress of the war though the coverage in a student newspaper, a newspaper of the Weekly Reader company which I think was called *Current Events*. I was in the seventh grade when the war with Germany ended, and Japan also surrendered that summer. The Weekly Reader newspaper during the school year of 1945–46 informed us about post-war efforts to consolidate progress toward world peace. I read about the founding of the United Nations. World leaders in America and Western Europe were optimistic that they had created an effective mechanism for world peace.

"There was virtually no science in the formal curriculum of the country school, other than a course in hygiene. But in *Current Events* I read about futuristic technologies that had been the by-product of wartime research. There were articles about atomic energy, jet propulsion, FM radio and even an invention that could relay pictures as well as sound from place to place over the air waves. Television seemed to be a prospect for the far future, but within five years most homes had a television set.

"But in 1945 radio was still the technology which was best in keeping America informed. Mrs. Kurtz brought her own radio on May 7, 1945, when the German military leadership signed a surrender document in a schoolhouse in Germany. A few day after the German surrender, Mrs. Kurtz spoke quietly with me and another seventh-grader. Our two other classmates would be excused for the remainder of the term as they were engaged in agricultural production. Since we also worked on farms, we were excused, as well. Although the war with

Germany was over, the farms of Richland Township were still needed to produce food to feed the world.

"When adults visited our isolated school they aroused great curiosity. Two visitors made a special impression. One was Dr. Paul Gruber, who was the official supervisor of our teachers. Dr. Gruber was the assistant superintendent of Bucks County Public Schools, and he was responsible for rating the teachers. We looked forward to his visits, which took place every couple of years. He was a cheerful man, and his visits were more those of a resource person than an inspector. Dr. Gruber still had a faint Pennsylvania Dutch accent, and when he came he conferred with the teacher, tested students' hearing with an audiometer, and taught by innovative techniques, such as 'casting out nines' as a way of proving addition problems.

"Less pleasant was a visit from our neighbor, the farmer who owned the land around the school. The farmer was gruff and did not have a good command of English. We had heard that he had immigrated from Central Europe, worked in the anthracite mines of the Coal Region of Pennsylvania, and made enough money to buy the dairy farm. We students who passed his farmhouse were afraid of him.

"He had an obsession about students trespassing on his property and had erected a nasty fence of wooden posts with perhaps six strands of barbed wire between the school yard and his pasture. He would yell when students crawled under the barbed-wire fence to retrieve a ball. We tried to be sure that he wasn't around when we sneaked into the pasture.

"But inevitably we would not only sneak under the fence but use the pasture as a playground. The farmer must have been watching from his barn, for one afternoon the door of the school flew open. The farmer vented his rage on Miss Mae, who tactfully steered him to the door and finally outside. We felt as if a thunderstorm had passed through the school. For some reason, he never chased us from the pasture again.

"Eighth-grade students in country schools were required to take a standardized test to determine if they would be eligible for entry into high school. The test took an entire day and was given at Shaw's School, another country school near Quakertown. I was given permission to ride my bicycle to Shaw's School, which was perhaps three miles from our home.

"I was impressed by the baseball diamond at Shaw's School. It was on the other side of the road from the school on property owned by the Willauer family. The baseball field had a wooden backstop, mowed grass, and regular bases. What a contrast with our playground! What a difference between the attitude of the Willauer family and that of our neighbor at Scholl's School!

"The two highest ranking students in the graduating class were given special recognition as valedictorian and salutatorian. I and a girl from the Shelly school were the co-salutatorians. There were four graduates from Scholl's School, another boy and two girls. There were about thirty-five graduates from the nine schools in the township.

"Graduation took place in late May in St. John's Lutheran Church in Rich-landtown. As one of the two tallest boys, I helped to lead the processional. I had not known most of my classmates from the other eight schools for very long, so there was not the feeling of nostalgia of subsequent graduation exercises. By the time that high school began again in September, some of my newly familiar classmates from the township left formal education for good as they could under the compulsory education rules of the time. But most of my classmates continued on to high school. Some dropped out along the way to high school graduation. Probably only 50 to 60 percent of those who graduated from the Richland Township schools in 1946 were members of the graduating class of Quakertown High School in 1950.

"In the fall of 1946, the school district provided buses. I took a bus to the high school. My brother, who was then in the fifth grade, continued in Scholl's School for two years, while my sister, who was in seventh grade, was transported by bus to the Tohickon School, about four miles away. It was the beginning of the end of the era of the one-room school of eight grades. There was to be a short transitional period, when the old one-room schools were used for two or three grades from an extended area. Busing made that possible. During the next decade, school reorganization was taking place, and plans were soon on the drawing boards for consolidated schools, so the old one-room schools could be replaced completely. The pre–World War II children had been served by the one-room schools, but the baby boom generation needed modern schools.

"In retrospect, I was fortunate to have the experiences of the one-room school. With millions of other country children I lived in an era and an institution which will never be replicated."

Themes

The topics of teachers, teaching methods, and discipline will be explored from a variety of interviews in Chapter 3. The perceived values of the "hidden curriculum" will be examined in Chapter 4.

This was the beginning of an era of universal secondary education. The eighth-grade tests were no longer selective. Although the students in the rural schools still took the eighth-grade examination in 1946, virtually all of the students passed and were eligible to enter high school, and a larger proportion of students went on to high school graduation by the post–World War II years.

In the two following stories, there will be further discussions of the transitional period during which the one-room schools were used as primary, intermediate, or middle school centers as students were bused while consolidated schools were being planned and built.

YOU CAN GO HOME AGAIN

> Give me the country school any time.
> —Carrie Frankenfield Horne

Carrie Frankenfield Horne, who became a highly respected teacher, had the unique experience of attending a two-room country school from 1904–12 and of returning to that same school as a teacher in 1947, after World War II. During the thirty-five years between her graduation from the country school and her return to the same school as a teacher, Mrs. Horne completed her teacher certification at Keystone State Normal School, taught in city schools, married, raised a family, became widowed, and returned to teaching in response to the post-World War II baby boom.

"I was a student at what was then known as the Fairmount School. Later it was called the Passer School. It was a two-room school. I started in 1904 in the primary school for my first four years, and then I 'graduated' into the big room and was there for four years.

"One of those four years my teacher was my own sister. That was a little difficult sometimes. I was sure to behave myself. Not only that but she was pretty hard on me when it came to final exams; she gave the final exams to us to enter grammar school. Once I was heartbroken because I had a perfect arithmetic paper but she took one point off. I couldn't understand why but then to ease my heart in the evening she told me she had to do it because I had missed the decimal point in one of the places so that was why.

"We studied reading, writing, arithmetic, physiology, geography, and spelling. We were strong on history, geography, and physiology. We had tablets but paper was kind of scarce so in the beginning we did a lot of our work on slates with slate pencils. We did a lot of work at the blackboard. The teacher might call up an entire class and give us assignments because it was simple for her to check our work on the blackboard.

"The desks were screwed into place in rows. We had four rows of desks in the room with a potbelly stove in the center and shields on the side of that potbelly stove so that in the wintertime when the stove had to be red hot they kind of shielded the people who sat closest to the stove. On real cold days when it was impossible to heat the entire building, the teacher could move benches up close to the stove so we'd all be warm.

"At that time I would judge that we had twenty-five to thirty pupils. When Springfield Township High School came into existence the upper grades were not quite so heavy because some of the children went to high school earlier than they had before. The students could go to high school as soon as they would pass an exam. Some of the teachers would let the youngsters double up on their work so that they could go to high school sooner. I think they must have given them some kind of test so that they got to high school very young. My sister

Fairmount (Passer) School in 1904. This is the school attended by Carrie Frankenfield as a student. Note the tower that was later removed. Photo reproduced courtesy of the Passer Community Association.

and my parents frowned on that and insisted that I have eight years at Passer before I went to high school. I think it was a good thing.

"In the primary room the teacher had a boxlike desk behind which she sat. One of her favorite punishments when youngsters were real bad was to stick them in that desk and they were just boxed in there.

"The school term began in early September but I think we only had seven months of school. School was finished by the end of April, because at that time the area was rural farming. The children were needed at home, even those whose fathers were like my father. He was not really a full-time farmer. But they had to grow their own food so there was work at home for the children.

"My sister started teaching at something like 40–45 dollars a month. She had done such an excellent job the first year that the school board increased her salary by a dollar a month. So they were not very well paid for the seven months that they taught. Their yearly pay was about three hundred dollars.

"I went into teaching because in those days it was really about the only thing a woman could do. I guess it was just drilled into me that being a teacher was a pretty fine thing because my father always made my sister feel that she had a wonderful calling. He tried to ingrain that into all of us.

"I went four years to Springfield Township High School. We studied Latin, English, history, math, geometry, physics, and biology. I don't believe that we had chemistry at all. We were not too far advanced in Latin. We had to keep meticulous notebooks in all of those subjects. Then I decided that I was going to go to the normal school. When I graduated from high school in 1916 the thing to do was to try to get a job as a teacher. In those days you could become a teacher by going to a normal school for a six-week summer session and then get a special teaching permit from the county superintendent. My sister took me to Keystone Normal [later renamed Kutztown State Teachers College] with that idea of enrolling me in the summer only. But the principal of Keystone urged her to try to get me through two years. I guess maybe he was anxious to see another two years of a Frankenfield, as my sister had gone there for two years and my brother had, ten years before.

"I lived in the dormitories at the normal school. They were very strict about coming home. I had to have a letter from my mother saying that I was allowed to come home on a weekend. I had to sign out when I left and sign in when I came in.

"I continued my study of Latin, more advanced than I had in high school. I did get geometry and trigonometry. I loved math very much, and I remember especially that we had quite an advanced math class, intense problems that we solved that seem ridiculous now.

"And of course there was teacher training. At that time the normal schools had what they called a model school. You got your training in that model school. You taught under supervision. They usually had a man and a woman supervisor, and you taught under them and got your rating. The man was noted for not giving any high grades. He was very stingy with his grades. I happened to be one of the people seated at his table in the dining room, because each table in the dining room had one professor at the table. I guess I was one of his special people, because he always called us that, and I did pull his highest grade.

"Then I got a normal certificate. That's what they called it. You had to teach for two years within the state of Pennsylvania and get the recommendation of the superintendent of schools of the county. There were no supervising principals then. If he recommended after two years that you had done a good job, you would get a permanent normal diploma certificate. In the beginning it was just a certificate entitling you to teach, but that normal diploma was really something, because it entitled you to teach in any room in the state of Pennsylvania about thirty subjects; starting with algebra and ending with zoology. I still have the certificate.

"When I graduated it was still during the time of World War I. Before I graduated there was a Mr. Snyder who was principal of the Washington School in Northampton Heights, which is now part of the Bethlehem School District. He came to the normal school hiring teachers, and I was to teach there in Northampton Heights. It was close enough to home that I felt that some arrangements could be made. One of the girls I could travel with was also hired to teach there. My sister at that time had gone back to teaching, so the three of us took in another girl. We had an apartment and lived together in Allentown. There was just a short commute to my school. I taught second grade in the Washington School.

"I taught there for two years, and then I got very bold, and went to see the superintendent of schools in the city of Allentown, because the pay was better there. My starting salary at Northampton Heights was fifty-five dollars a month, but we did have a ten-month term. Because we were so close to Bethlehem Steel and the war was going on, the Steel was hiring at enormous salaries. The school board offered us a bonus of twenty-five dollars if we would stay until the end of the school year. I would have gotten something like seventy-two dollars a month. But Allentown at that time had a permanent salary schedule, which I was anxious to have. I nervously approached the superintendent. He asked me why I wanted to teach in Allentown, and I told him that I had lived in Allentown for two years. So I was hired to teach in Allentown at $105 a month.

"The school to which I was assigned was the Jefferson School which was in South Allentown near the Good Shepherd Home. But I never taught in the main building, because things were very crowded in those days. I started teaching in a temporary building on the playground. I shared the room with another teacher. She went in from eight to ten in the morning. I came in with another group of children from ten to twelve; she came back at twelve and taught till two with her group. I came back at two with my group until four. That was a kind of a mess; so finally they decided to go to full half days. I taught for half days in that building. Then they bought a property with a house on it. They converted that house into classrooms. I taught downstairs and the other girl was upstairs, so that we were both on full time.

"I taught just second grade. We had a music supervisor and we had a supervisor of athletics. We had a general supervisor, who was very, very strict. The teachers were all women, and they ignored the principal of the building, but listened to the supervisor, a woman who had charge of all the elementary subjects in all the elementary schools. She would come from one school to another to supervise.

"After teaching in Allentown I got married and moved with my husband to Springfield Township in Bucks County for maybe three or four years, and then we moved down to Whitemarsh Township, a suburb of Philadelphia, in Montgomery County. For sixteen years we lived down there. In the meantime I had a daughter, and I felt it was my duty to stay home with her. But then we moved back to the country and took up my mother's old home because my husband and I had inherited it after her death. It was our dream to live back here because we were both raised here. We moved back here and before we were even settled in the home we were asked to take teaching jobs. At that time they were having a difficult time in Wimmer's School, in Richland Township. They asked me to come to teach. After so many years I was really scared. But my husband said I had wanted to do it, so I did take Wimmer's School and I enjoyed my work there. I had been away from teaching for about twenty years, so it was quite a challenge.

"Wimmer's was a one-room school, with grades one to eight, with a big fat stove in the corner that had to be tended like any other stove. We did have a pump with water. Unfortunately my husband died that March, so it was a very difficult year for me. But also I was very grateful and thankful that I was teaching, because, for one reason or other, children can be very understanding and helpful. Those kids at Wimmer's School were that. So they helped me through the year.

"Then after a year in which I lived with my daughter near Conshohocken and taught fifth and sixth grades there, I came back home in 1947.

"I taught seventh and eighth grades in the Passer School where I had been a student. I had a wonderful time. It was still a two-room school. By that time they had consolidated the rural schools of Springfield Township by transporting the students to different schools. In Passer we had fifth and sixth grades in one room and seventh and eighth in the other.

"The improvements weren't that great except we had electric, and thanks to the Sunday school, we had an organ and a piano. The stove was still there. The children were hauled to the school on buses from all of the area.

"We opened school one fall and I had forty-four youngsters in my room. The teacher in the other room also had fourty-four. We staggered time on the playground. We still didn't have enough playground space but we had a very active PTA. The PTA bought a three-acre tract to the north of the school. The school board loaned the money to us. After picking up all the stones, we managed to have two or three ball diamonds, so that we could have three good ball games going at one time. We sold seeds and we sold other things to get our own playground equipment, which was not given to us by the school district.

Passer School in 1950. By 1950, the old Fairmount School was called the Passer School. This photo shows the school as it was when Carrie Frankenfield Horne taught seventh and eighth grade there in the 1950s. Photo reproduced courtesy of the Passer Community Association.

"By 1953, several townships had consolidated to form a jointure. They built Palisades Junior-Senior High School. In the middle of the 1952–53 school term we were ready to move to the new school. We opened school in the morning in Passer with our regular opening exercises. We had everything packed. Then we moved over. I moved to the new high school with my seventh graders.

"That was a difficult day. In fact, unashamedly I cried. A lot of the children were crying, too. We had a very happy experience together. In fact, I would say that those years at Passer were the highlights of my teaching career. I loved it there.

"At the junior-senior high school I did departmental work for about two years. I didn't like it. I was used to closeness with my children. Then we had so many youngsters failing because of the sudden change. I was talked into taking a special class, a remedial class. I did that remedial work for about four years. I kept the same group for two years. Then our high school enrollment increased and we had a lot of youngsters that were not of the mental ability to face regular high school classes, so I finally ended up teaching a special class. They were in my room for seventh and eighth grades. After eighth grade they left my room. If I felt they were at all fit they had to enter regular ninth grade and it was a hard thing. We tried very hard to get a senior high special class. One was started after I left. I remember one year I tried to force it by keeping some of my eighth graders—holding them for another year, teaching them the regular subjects, and letting them go to other classes for other things. But that was a hard year because I had twenty-five youngsters with three grades to handle. I tried to find something that they could do well, so that they would have a feeling of accomplishment. I wanted them to feel, 'I can do something, and I can do it well.' Many of them had artistic talents. I did a lot of varied things with them.

"I think that teaching was quite different in the high school. There were very few youngsters that you could get close to, and for the first time, when I got over there, I experienced a gang that would stick together. If you punished one, you had difficulty with the whole gang. This was not true in the country schools, at least in the country schools in which I taught, because if there were two or three who banded together, you could get some of your good kids to help you disperse the gang and to back you in disciplining them. This was not true when you had a larger gang in the high school setup. I was uneasy. I was unhappy because I was not close enough to the youngsters. I had too many students for special education. I had twenty or more students every year.

"On the other hand, I didn't have the responsibilities of the country school such as keeping the outside toilets sanitary and safe, and the fires going. I was lucky when I taught at Passer because the husband of the teacher in the other room took care of the fire in her room, and he offered to take care of mine.

"When I taught at Wimmer's School, I would let the fire go out on Friday, and then my husband would go over on a Sunday afternoon to get it going, so by Monday it was all right. In fact there was a rule at one time that the school board had made, that a teacher could not leave the country school unless the fire was completely out on a Friday. You had to be there early on Monday to make sure the building was warm. You had to start fresh and be there early.

"In fact, you had better be there early for a lot of things, because if there was the slightest bit of snow, or ice, you might be delayed. I remember one morning when it was especially icy. The school that I taught in Passer was built on a little ridge. I got down to the bottom of the hill, and I thought how am I going to get up it this morning, straight up on either side. Practically on hands and knees I got up the hill, and I thought to myself, 'Well, you made it again.' But usually I had the boys leave a bucket of ashes right inside the door, because the buses would come in and slide, so that the children might practically slide under the wheels.

"We were closer in the country school. In those days we were still allowed our opening exercises. Sometimes the two rooms would get together to share our opening exercises. My youngsters loved to sing. We could sing in the morning as long as we wanted.

"We had to organize a safety patrol, because there was a great deal of interchange of buses. We got to be a central place for the interchange of buses, of children changing from one bus to another. It got to be quite a mix-up; so we organized a safety patrol. We had a wonderful safety patrol. The first captain of it was Mr. Willard Wilson. Later it was my privilege to be a fellow teacher with him at Palisades. He did a wonderful job as well as did the entire safety patrol. They reported youngsters that did not follow rules, and they, after consulting with me, meted out punishment. After we got our playground the favorite punishment was picking up so many stones, because there were millions of stones.

"I should give credit to Mark Mease. He was a bus driver, but he was also a big help. When the grate broke in the stove he had it fixed. If a stray dog came to the school he took it along with him and did things like that. He did a lot for us. I think that he was the first to own his own bus in Palisades.

"A Sunday School Union shared the Passer School building with the school. That Sunday school organization was actually started in the year 1851. I think my grandfather, Simon Frankenfield, was responsible as one of the organizers. There were no churches closely available. He was considered to be an evangelical preacher and he organized the Sunday school. They kept very minute and sometimes funny records. They usually kept a record of the weather and the fact that there was no Sunday school on a certain date because the roads were too muddy.

"They must have met in the log schoolhouse that first stood near Passer. They must have met in the Passer School where I taught from the first time that it was used as a public school. One of the many nice things about having the Sunday school meet in there was the fact that they wanted an organ, and the school had no organ or piano, so they got an organ, and we then had an organ available. Later on the Sunday school got a piano which we could use. The Sunday school had also put in a Delco light system, and had wired things up so that they had lights for the picnics. The Sunday school picnic was a big affair in the days when there weren't so many things going on.

"The Sunday school did a great deal, I think, to bring the school along. The school building was a community center. When anything went wrong in the community, when there was a death, or something in the school (because there were quite a number of young people who died who were in the school), the neighborhood just kind of joined together and did something for them. The schoolhouse was a meeting place for anything at all.

"Our country school library had whatever books the teachers could afford to buy, and they scrimped and scratched to get everything together that they could, because children loved to read. Also they got books that were donated to them. I remember when I went to school, we had a series of books called *Pepper and Holly Grove*. There was a whole series of those books. With the money they had, the teacher could buy one book a year. I had read everything in the school library. One evening, when my sister was my teacher, I had my nose buried in a book at home. We had company that night. She said something about my being a bookworm. She said, 'What are you reading now?' and she looked at the book. She was horrified because it was an adult book which was not for children. Someone had donated it. So they had to weed out some of the books.

"When I was a teacher in the Passer School the students signed the books in and out. We had a pretty extensive library. Because some of the youngsters would want to know what a book was about, I asked the children to write a short summary of the books that they checked out and put the report on a card file. We kept the file so the other children could read the report as a preview of the book. Whenever any of the children did that they would give me the card, and I would give them credit. It was sort of like a short book report. It stimulated reading. There was always an emphasis upon good reading.

"I often think about why they switched to the consolidated schools. There were advantages, of course. Sometime ago I wrote an article on health, then in the old-time schools, and now, how conditions are. Because the one thing that every rural teacher was frightened of, always, was a serious injury to a youngster. We were at a disadvantage because we were so isolated. You couldn't leave the youngsters to get to a telephone.

"During the last couple of years that I taught at Passer, I had a telephone, and it was a wonderful thing to have because I was in direct touch with the principal's office. If there was a discipline case in my room, or in the room next door, that I felt should be handled by the principal, I could call him in front of the children, which was very effective. It was a big help.

"I loved the children in both the country school and the high school, and they responded likewise. I had a boy that hated school. He got into my special class at Palisades and for some reason or other he and I clicked. About three or four months ago he stopped in here at my home, and he was telling me about what he was doing. He's now a forest ranger, and he was telling me about his children, showing me pictures. It's very rewarding.

"Someone once asked me if I'd like to go back to teaching, while I was still capable, what would I say if I had a choice between a country school, or a well-built departmentalized school. I said, 'Give me the country school any time.'"

Themes

Carrie Frankenfield was from a family of teachers, so she went into teaching with some advantages. Other young teachers at that same period entered teaching by taking a summer course after high school. Like her older sister, Carrie Frankenfield Horne had a two-year program at the teacher preparation institution at Kutztown, Pennsylvania. At the time she attended it was called Keystone Normal School. Later it was called Kutztown State Teacher's College, and it is presently Kutztown University of Pennsylvania. She had practice teaching as a part of her preparation program and qualified for a "Normal" certificate. The experiences of other teachers in becoming certified with a Normal certificate are included in Chapter 3.

At present there is a universal school term of at least 180 days. But school boards in the period prior to the Depression had some degree of local autonomy in setting the school term. Carrie Frankenfield attended school for a school term of seven months, or about 140 days, in the rural area. When as Miss Frankenfield she taught in the urban schools of Northampton Heights and Allentown at the time of World War I the school term was ten months, or about two hundred days. As pay was by the month, the length of the school term made a big difference. The agriculturally based school term is described by others in Chapter 3. Games played and the influence of voluntarism will be discussed further in Chapter 4.

The level of voluntarism shown at the Passer School was remarkable. There was cooperation with the Sunday school, which brought some benefits in the use of the organ and a piano, but the prime example was in the purchase of three acres of land next to the school, which was converted into ball fields.

FROM ONE-ROOM SCHOOL TO THE CONSOLIDATED SCHOOL

> The consolidated school was so much more structured. Not to say that the one-room schools didn't have structure, but it was a flexible structure.
>
> —Beverly Kehs Purcell

Beverly Kehs Purcell had been an elementary school student during the early 1950s, when modern consolidated schools replaced the traditional eight-grade, one-room school. During this period of change, school buses were used to transport children between the old country schools. The typical plan was for the schools to have two or three grades of students in each of the old one-room

Carrie Frankenfield Horne. Mrs. Horne is shown at two stages of her career. The photo on the left shows her as she graduated from Kutztown State Normal School, when she began her teaching career. The other photo was taken while she was a teacher at the Passer School. Photos reproduced courtesy of her daughter, Mrs. Robert Heiland.

schools. One plan was for a cluster of three schools. One schoolhouse would hold primary grades (first to third), another would house the intermediate grades (four to six), and the other would serve seventh- and eighth-graders. But the schools of the early 1950s were inadequate to serve the first wave of baby boomers. Sometimes modifications in the grade structure had to be made during the school term, as Mrs. Purcell indicates.

"I guess I went with the first generation of baby boomers. I know there were at least four grades in the Three-Mile Run School, which is where I went to first and second grade. After the second grade there were two grades in each of the three buildings.

"I got to the one-room school by bus. One time the road was really snowy. We lived on Hill Road and it is aptly named. It is hills and turns and everything else. The driver got the bus up to the top of the hill, and it was so slippery that he made all the kids get off the bus and walk to the bottom of the hill. He took the bus down by himself. There was no guard rail, no anything. He was afraid for our safety. So after that, he said, 'Listen, children, if the roads are like this again, if you are going to school, you come down to the bottom of the hill because I'm not going to take the bus up that hill.'

"I don't remember much about the first teachers. I had Mrs. Freed in the fourth grade. Mrs. Freed had sort of an impact, because she was one of the first teachers who started giving me the 'Beverly is not working up to her potential' type thing. She sat me behind a screen for a couple of weeks. I had already heard the fourth-grade lessons when I was in the third grade, so I didn't have to pay attention because I knew the lessons.

"The transition to the consolidated school was in the spring of the fifth grade. The consolidated school was different. There were all kinds of rules that we never had at the one-room school. Teachers in one-room schools were pretty much autonomous. I assume they had rules they had to go by, but we weren't aware of them. If the teacher decided that, 'You guys were really good today, I'll let you have an extra fifteen minutes for recess,' they could do that. There was a lot of freedom in the one-room school that we lost in the consolidated school. In the consolidated school, if you were having a real good lesson, a teachers would feel, 'Oh, why does the bell have to ring now? The kids are into it, I'm into it, everything is going well.' But in the one-room school they didn't have to stop. If everybody was working well together they could keep on going.

"Plus, I would assume that teacher-wise it had its advantages and disadvantages. The teacher was the only adult in the school. I don't remember anyone ever getting hurt in the one-room school other than bruised knees, or whatever, but there were no phones in case of an emergency. A lot of the schools had no neighbors.

"It wasn't a rich school. Nobody dressed up. Of course, back then nobody had designer jeans. You weren't allowed to wear jeans, anyway. Jeans back in those days had rivets in the pockets. You were afraid to sit on something and scratch it. We had dress codes. If it was cold, you could wear a pair of pants under a dress. Girls always wore dresses. And no cleats on shoes, because cleats would spoil the floors.

"Once a year we had to help oil the floor. We began by sweeping the floor, to get the dirt out. I remember putting the oil on the floor and sweeping more. It sure made a mess when you sat on the floor. You got all the oil on you.

"One of the neat things about having the stove in the room was when we'd bring a potato in wrapped in aluminum foil. We'd come in the morning and throw our potato on a shelf on the inside of the stove, and we'd have hot baked potatoes for lunch. It was wonderful, really great. Plus, in the wintertime we had what we called pop sticks, because the milk that sat out on the porch would freeze and pop the little paper tops off, and you'd have these cones of cream that you got to sit and eat.

"We had outdoor plumbing. There was no running water inside at all. There was a pump outside. We weren't supposed to play with it because you'd get your feet all wet. Every year someone would knock over the outhouse. The girls' outhouse would be knocked over on Mischief Night. It was always turned over on Mischief Night. The girls always went to the outhouse in sets of twos. That was probably why women always go to the bathroom in pairs. You got to go in twos, so one would stand guard at the door to make sure that none of the boys got in while you were there.

"I have no idea about how large the playground was because we would play in the fields around the school. I'm not sure that we were supposed to. I know one day we had been out playing, and we were far enough away that we didn't hear the bell. We wandered back sometime later. Karen Roeder and I used to hang out all the time when we were growing up. She was my best friend then. We were out playing 'horses,' as we always did. It was real neat being a girl because you had this high belt in back, and of course you always got into trouble because your mother said, 'You're playing horses again, weren't you? Your belt's torn,' You know, 'giddy up.' We were out, playing in the woods or something, and we didn't hear the bell. One of us finally said, 'Seems like an awfully long recess; do you think we should go back?' Well, we wound up being put in the corner. We were way late coming back.

"We all played baseball at the one-room school. Somebody always had a ball game going. One of the problems that we ran into when we went to the consolidated school was when the head teacher decided that young ladies did not play baseball and we weren't allowed to play.

"The teachers had to be creative in finding things for the children to do at lunch hour and recess. They had to be. In retrospect, now having been a parent and involved in different groups, I have the utmost respect for them. I really do. I didn't consider becoming a teacher myself. At this age there is no way that I'd be a teacher. I don't have the patience for people who don't want to learn. And I was one of the biggest people who had a problem in school!

"I think it would probably be very enlightening for today's teachers to have to do some type of internship in an old school setting where they had eight grades, or six grades, or even two grades, and keep track of them by themselves. I think if a lot of today's teachers would go back they would say, 'We have it made: teaching today is easy.' I can do nothing but give the teachers a lot of credit just to keep that many kids going. I have a warm feeling about having gone to a one-room school. The only thing I had a problem with was my accelerated program while I was still in the lower grades. I'd go to classes with the upper grades, and then the next year I didn't have to do anything because I knew the lessons already. Except that only one year of that classroom was an accelerated class. The rest of it was repeating. That was a bore. But the experience in the one-room school reinforced my tendency to be an underachiever in school later on.

"As a case in point, I can remember sitting in algebra class in the ninth grade in the senior high. The teacher stood at the board and explained the concepts behind one type of an algebraic equation and I would listen, understand it, and goof off the rest of the class. Which puts me in mind of the little screen that Mrs. Freed used to put me behind away from the rest of the class. Because while I was goofing off, of course, some kids that weren't disciplined enough to not pay attention to what I was doing would goof off with me and then they would flunk the test while I passed it. So I can't help but think that it had a lot to do with my work habits that I learned in the one-room school.

"However, we did learn the fundamentals. They would be hammered into your head. I notice that with my children they didn't stress the multiplication tables. We had hours and hours of drill. In recent years in teaching reading they decided that phonetics was the way to go. Sound the words. My son has graduated from high school, but still spells phonetically.

"The interesting thing about the one-room schools is that they were really looked down upon as very primitive, as being backward, by many people at that time. The change in people's thinking is interesting, because then it was seen to be a great step forward to have the consolidated school, the bigger schools. They were more modern, you could do so much more. But people now say such positive things about the one-room schools.

"After the schools were consolidated the teachers weren't by themselves. A music teacher came in and an art teacher. I guess the regular teachers in the consolidated school had a lot more time to themselves for what they wanted to do. They got a break from us.

"In the consolidated school it was much more regulated because you had a bell that said, 'Okay, now stop teaching math, start teaching English,' or 'it's time for recess.' The consolidated school was so much more structured. Not to say that the one room-school didn't have structure, but it was a flexible structure. But the teachers were resourceful, and they adapted to the consolidated school.

"I remember that at that time they didn't have vaccinations for every little childhood disease around, and you were quarantined for measles, mumps, and chicken pox. I remember when the Salk vaccine first came out. I remember having sugar cubes with pink junk on it, and running into some children who had a mild case of polio because they hadn't gotten the vaccine when they should have. We had a spell of scarlet fever, and several of my friends were out for a long time. I had a mild case of scarlet fever back then. They tested the water at the school. That was scary, because the well was probably polluted, and we had been drinking from it."

Themes

By the 1950s the one-room schools were understood to be on their way out. Rural school districts were able to come up with an intermediate step by using busing to allow individual schools to serve just a few grade levels, as was described by Carrie Horne. But the population growth from the baby boom was such that modifications to the assignment of grade levels had to be made almost yearly in order to keep ahead of the population bubble. Where the single teacher in a one-room school of the past could keep track of students who were accelerated, this apparently did not happen in the case of Beverly Kehs (Purcell). She ended up with curriculum repetition that she did not feel she needed. This was one of the few cases where there was a complaint about repetition. Virtually all of the others whom we interviewed felt that it was a good thing.

The comparison between the less structured school day in the one-room school and the highly organized consolidated school demonstrates the trade-off that was made when teachers had to conform to the electronic clock. Teachers had the benefit of specialist teachers in art and music and physical education, but lost a good bit of flexibility in managing the school day. The final chapter of this volume contains a case study in which a school superintendent recalls the events in which several small school districts were consolidated into one large school district, as well as comparisons between the advantages and disadvantages of the one-room school experience.

3

Teaching and Learning in the One-Room School

> In rural America, . . . local communities operated schools and dedicated instruction to local needs. The curriculum of rural schools in the late 19th and early 20th centuries was often limited to character training and basic literacy and numeracy.
> —Alan J. DeYoung and Barbara Kent Lawrence ("On Hoosiers, Yankees, and Mountaineers," *Phi Delta Kappan*, October 1995, 107)

The one-room school was first of all an institution with the public responsibility of instilling literacy in the emerging generation. By the twentieth century a professional class of educators was assigned the responsibility of carrying out the task of school teaching. A curriculum had been developed and was drawn from formal textbooks that school boards purchased and teachers utilized.

This chapter deals with the formal side of the one-room school experience. Teachers taught, and when they taught they personalized the learning of the basics. This chapter probes the memories of some of the former students and teachers in one-room schools about the teaching of the basics and the character of the teachers.

TEACHERS

> And I am firm in my belief that a teacher lives on and on through his students. I will live if my teaching is inspirational, good, and stands firm for good values and character training. Tell me how can good teaching ever die? Good teaching is forever and the teacher is immortal.
> —Jesse Stuart (*The Thread that Runs So True*, 1958, x)

John Cartwright, a respected educator who served as superintendent of the Allentown, Pennsylvania, school district and later as professor of education at Lehigh University during the middle decades of this twentieth century, was once asked, "What is the best education?" His reply was, "A one-room school, if you have the best teacher."

The teacher made the difference between a good and poor one-room school. The personality, character, and expertise of individual teachers were the most important attributes of teachers and the key to their effectiveness. The teachers' influence in the schoolroom was amplified because they taught literally everything. In the contemporary single-grade elementary classrooms there are specialist teachers to teach art, music, and physical education. Principals, librarians, guidance counselors, reading specialists, and learning support teachers provide backup services to elementary school classroom teachers today. The teacher in the one-room school had none of these human resources, and, of course, no computers. They were the "general practitioners" of education, just as the country doctors were the general practitioners of medicine during the same era.

Of course, the teachers in one-room schools varied in quality and competence. Early in the twentieth century some were hired at age eighteen with no formal preparation other than having completed high school and having attended a country school themselves. Others had completed a summer session or even a two-year program of normal school training. Some had prepared in a liberal arts college; others, after taking a bachelor's degree, had done their certification studies. Some were incompetent; some were superb. Our interviewees generally remembered the good ones better than the mediocre ones. We had asked them to recall their teachers and to describe their best ones.

EXEMPLARY TEACHERS

Several teachers were exemplary, in the opinions of their students and peers. In the previous chapter the contributions of Lloyd (Poppy) Yoder were described by his niece, Ruth Hackman, who was one of his students. Carrie Frankenfield Horne, whose story was also told in Chapter 2, was a legend in the rural schools that later made up the Palisades School District. Pupils in Shaw's School, in Richland Township during the 1920s, 1930s, and 1940s had the benefit of the teaching of Laura Strunk, who touched the lives of many students. During her entire tenure at Shaw's School, the school was overcrowded, having forty to fifty students each year as the norm.

Another great teacher was Florence Fluck, who taught in Richland Township and Haycock Township over a long career. She too was a legendary figure and a source of inspiration for her students and peers. Miss Alice Paul was another exemplary teacher whose life was devoted to her students. She taught in a one-room school in East Rockhill Township.

These great teachers, among others, shared certain characteristics. They were good disciplinarians while still seen as having a heart. They were kind to their students and interested in them as individuals. They were innovative in their teaching techniques and demonstrated a lifetime enthusiasm for learning as well as teaching.

Clara Willauer Kipp attended Shaw's School, graduating from the eighth grade in 1921. She recalled that there were anywhere from forty to forty-five students in the school when she attended. "My teacher in grades seven and eight was Mrs. Strunk. We had a lot of respect for Mrs. Strunk. She was very strict, but she was a lovable teacher as far as I was concerned. I think she was interested in everybody. She was really interested that I go to high school."

Ed Fox attended the same school. "Mrs. Laura Strunk was the teacher. She was well liked and a fine teacher. She was like a second mother to all the pupils there."

Galen Lowman reported upon an innovation by Mrs. Strunk. "Mrs. Strunk was a kindly, motherly person. She was a pioneer in a hot lunch program. We had the first hot lunch program in the area, as far as I know.

"We had a kerosene range in the corner, and we'd have hot chocolate. Toward lunchtime the older girls would get it started. Then they would watch the stove and serve the youngsters their cups of cocoa. Mr. Erwin Landis had a dairy farm about a quarter of a mile away, and they would bring milk from his farm. We sold seeds to raise money to buy the chocolate. Toward spring, when the money ran out, the families nearby would bring soup. We still carried our own sandwiches, but this gave us a hot lunch."

Catherine Benner Bleam told this story about Mrs. Strunk. "We didn't know where Mrs. Strunk was during recess. We found her in the coal bin mending a little kid's trousers that he'd torn. She had taken him in the coal bin, took off his trousers, and she was sitting there mending them."

Good teachers had to be concerned about the hygiene of their students. Mrs. Bleam told another story about Mrs. Strunk. "One time it was funny. There was an outbreak of lice and she made everybody go up front and she was examining their heads. There was one big boy there and she said, 'Fred, you have a regular cootie garage there. Now you go home.' And he says, 'Oh, thank you.' He was tickled pink that he had to go home."

Sometimes Mrs. Strunk taught a lesson out of school as well as in school, as Mrs. Bleam recalls. "There was a woman who lived in one of the row houses that we used to pass on the way to school. It was said that she was a whore. So us kids [sic] would walk past her house and shout, 'Hi, you old whore.' Mrs. Strunk found out about it. She came down and met us before we got to the woman's house and marched us past there and we weren't allowed to say a word. We were punished, so we didn't do that again."

Ruth Clemmer Giering had attended Tohickon School with Mrs. Florence Fluck as the teacher. "I had Mrs. Florence Fluck as my teacher from about 1928 or 1929 until 1937. She was terrific. She had more than 30 students in eight grades. People loved and respected Mrs. Fluck. She always tried to have you up-to-date. She had meetings of the Parent-Teacher Association. We had Halloween parties; always something that didn't make the school days monotonous."

Anna Neamand was a neophyte teacher in the 1930s in the Wimmer School. She regarded Mrs. Fluck as her mentor. "I can't help but say what a help Mrs. Florence Fluck was to me. She was the kindest, most enthusiastic person that I ever met. She was just endless in her assistance to me and very generous to everybody. She shared anything she would have, any material, any ideas, anything to help you. When you wanted, she was always there. I was glad that I began teaching with her as a mentor."

Shaw's School students in the late 1920s. Mrs. Laura Strunk taught at Shaw's School for more than thirty years, often with an enrollment of forty or more students. In this photo she has fifty-one students. Photo reproduced courtesy of her son, Robert E. Strunk.

Mrs. Lamar Feikel commented upon the enthusiasm of Mrs. Fluck even decades after her active teaching career. "Mrs. Fluck was the ultimate teacher. I went to see her about two weeks before she went into the nursing home where she passed away, and one of her last questions was, 'How are the kids doing in school?' She was always the teacher, a very caring teacher, and anybody around here that knew her will tell you that. She was really a prize. She had been in and out of nursing homes in her last years. She was ninety-two when she passed away, but up until she was eighty-eight or eighty-nine she was just as youthful as you or I."

Kay Fox had attended the Rock Wild School in East Rockhill Township. We asked who her favorite teacher was. "Miss Paul, of course. She was a dear person. She loved her children. She loved her teaching. She enjoyed every moment of her life and we all loved her. She was very good to us."

Kay Fox reported that some of Miss Paul's former students wanted to do something special for Miss Paul on her eighty-fifth birthday. This would have been at least twenty years after her active career.

"It was Miss Paul's eighty-fifth birthday, and she lived to be in her nineties. Most of the graduates were still around here, and we thought we wanted to do something for her, so we had a 'This Is Your Life, Miss Paul' night for her down at the old school. We put up a curtain, and a lot of her former pupils got behind the curtain and, as you remember the program on television, they could ask questions and we'd write up little things from the past. I wrote the story about the night we spent at her house rehearsing for the Christmas play, and how we were angels. And she recognized me after all that time! I hadn't spoken to her for about twenty-five or thirty years, but she remembered my voice, and she remembered the night my sister and I had spent there at her place."

A BAD APPLE

Those students who had teachers such as Miss Paul or Mrs. Fluck were extremely fortunate. Evelyn Hendricks Potter recalled a very bad experience with a male teacher. "In second grade we had a man by the name of Mr. H. Oh, he was a villain! He was naughty, a very nasty man. He liked the older girls. There were not only stories; there was evidence that he had misbehaved.

"It was through my older brother and I that we had gone home to our parents and said, 'Mr. H. was doing this, and Mr. H was doing that.' So my father investigated, and they dismissed Mr. H. We saw him feel those girls at places where he shouldn't.

"Where you went into the school there was a little vestibule. On the one side would be shelves where we put our lunch boxes and on the other side were racks where we would hang our outer garments. Well, he would take these older girls out there in that little room. We could see him actually feel the girls.

"I think that the country folks at that time were very, very strict, and we had moved up from the town so maybe we were a little more sophisticated, and maybe my parents were aware. I don't think those girls would have dared tell their parents that Mr. H. did anything like that, even suggest that there could be something wrong, because for parents at that time the teacher was God.

"He would beat up on the children. He used to on my brother, and I remember screaming, 'You let my brother alone.' Tears would be rolling down my

Wimmer's School, 1937–38. This photo shows the enrollment in Wimmer's School during Miss Anna Neamand's third year of teaching. Photo reproduced courtesy of Miss Anna Neamand.

cheeks. Oh, it was sad. He had a big round, heavy stick, and then my brother would curl underneath the seat of the desk in front of his and Mr. H. would beat him up in there and really pound against him."

A teacher such as Mr. H. was a nightmare for parents and the school board. He had the authority of his position, and apparently used the isolation of the school to exercise sexual harassment. The only protection for the children was their ability to report to their parents. In this case, the parents took action. Fortunately, this was the only case that was reported to us of behavior such as this by a teacher.

A VARIETY OF TEACHERS

In some cases, the student in a particular school would have a variety of teachers over a period of years. Glenn Haring had six different teachers in his eight years at the Central School in Richland Township. He felt that there were substantial differences in the strengths and weaknesses of teachers.

"Academically the country school children did well when they went to high school. But there was always a weak field. Supposing you had a teacher with all eight grades, and supposing that teacher was weak in math. After all, he or she could not be strong in every subject. That would reflect on the children when they went into the high school because the kids in town had had different teachers for different subjects in the seventh and eighth grades. The specialization was not there in the one-room schools."

Robert Tarantino had several different teachers in his years in the California School. He compared their personalities. "I was born in 1907 and started school about 1914. I went to the California School. There were never under forty students there. Sometimes it was up to fifty or fifty-four students.

"My graduating [eighth-grade] teacher was the outstanding teacher. You know I never went home unless I walked home with her. She had to walk two miles into Quakertown. I had a crush on her. Most of the time I would wait for her after school. She was a wonderful person. She was a commonsense person. She died in a car accident. They were going around a curve; the door opened and she was killed. When we schoolchildren heard that, it was awful."

Robert Tarantino reflected the common acceptance of corporal punishment in his comparison of two male teachers. He accepted the use of the stick as a part of the teacher's authority. "My last teacher was Mr. R. He was one of the best teachers. He was at the school for sixteen years. He knew how to teach and could handle the pupils too. He was excellent. The first day of school he gave me a lickin' because I was showing a deck of cards to some boys. He said, 'Robert, put those cards away.' I said something smart and I started to put them away. He took me on the platform and gave me a lickin' right off the bat. And I needed it. That was the end of it and set a good example for the others. He was nice.

"The one who was really mean was Mr. S. He would give you a lickin' every day if you needed it. He was really severe. Two boys stayed in after school to be punished. The next morning the stick was broken in pieces on the platform. Then we talked to the boys. They were big, big, boys, and they had black and blue marks on their legs. He didn't beat them when the rest of us were there."

CONDITIONS AND DUTIES OF TEACHING

It was far from an easy job, and it had duties and obligations beyond belief. The teacher had no private life. She was watched jealously for any weakness of character.
—John Steinbeck (*East of Eden*, 1952, 170)

Melvin Mack recalled the many diverse tasks of his first teaching experience in a one-room school at Tylersport, near Souderton in Montgomery County, Pennsylvania, in 1935–37. This was during the Depression when teaching jobs were very difficult to obtain. "I started to teach at only ninety dollars a month, eight months. That was the going rate. End of May school stopped, and we'd come back right after Labor Day. So I taught for two years like that with no increase.

"Another thing was important. You had to keep what was called a state register, recording presence and absence of children, their names, in a big book. Then you had to count up the days of attendance, the days of membership. So it became a little bit of a mathematical problem. At the end of the month you went to the school board meeting with your register and turned it over to the school board secretary. He signed it and gave me my pay check.

"At the same time you had to take care of the fire, because I had a stove right in the middle with wood to start it and then coal to burn. I was dependent on the eighth-grade boys to go out and bring the coal in. I let my fire go out on the weekend, but some teachers had somebody in the neighborhood come in and keep the fire going, especially if you had flowers or an aquarium. But I took my flowers home each Friday night.

"Then we had to worry about water. We got our water from a farm, which was about three hundred yards away. Somebody would have to go up there with an open bucket, and then bring it back and put it into a cooler. We had one cup. Later on we asked each student to bring his own cup and hung them up on nails, when we got more health conscious."

Mary Hager Dietz told about the hospitality of families to teachers when she was a student at the Tohickon School in the period from 1914–21. "When I went to school the teacher used to stay overnight. I remember my teacher stayed out at our place more than once. She lived out in the country, and she was walking. If the weather was bad maybe she'd tell a family she'd stay at their house the next night. Everybody was excited; they wanted the teacher to stay, but she wasn't expected to stay at every house. We were close to the school."

There were restrictions upon the social life of teachers, particularly women teachers. Mary Strock recalled when she began teaching in 1938, "I taught five years in the one-room schoolhouse near Pleasant Valley in Springfield Township, teaching two years after I was married. But when you got a job you had to promise not to get married, not to be seen in a hotel, not even accompanied by a man, and to be sure you'd work in a church—teaching Sunday school or something. You could not go into a hotel which had a bar, even with your father.

"It was understood that we weren't allowed to smoke, although I can't recall that it was mentioned. But then, I was never one who smoked, so maybe they knew me. All the school directors knew me. I knew all of them. I had to. I went to see all of them to be interviewed for the teaching job. "

In some school districts the school board had a policy that they would not employ married women, although, as Mary Strock reported, she was unmarried when employed, but became married after three years on the job.

There were various rationales for this policy. Perhaps the most usual was the belief that if a woman were married, she would not be able to devote herself to teaching as much as an unmarried woman. Another was the belief that in a marriage the male should be the breadwinner.

Policies were influenced by social conditions. For example, because women could find lucrative employment in the wartime industries, many male and female teachers left teaching during World War I. Carrie Horne had spoken of the incentives to work in Bethlehem Steel, for example. Local school districts had to raise teacher salaries in order to retain teachers. But after the war, many urban schools districts would not hire married women.

Clara Willauer Kipp read from a newspaper article that described the policy of one school board after World War I. "At a meeting of the Reading School Board a resolution was adopted that any female teacher now employed in the Reading Schools who marries after May 1, 1923, must resign. During the war a number of married women were employed as teachers; some of them are still on duty. They will not be disturbed. But it is intended to engage only unmarried teachers in the future."

This policy worked to the advantage of the country schools in the long run. The urban schools could enforce such a policy in the first three or four decades of the century, long before the current woman's movement, because they paid substantially more than rural schools. As Mary Strock told us, although it was understood that some rural school districts had a policy to hire only unmarried women, the policy was not enforced strictly, particularly when good incumbent teachers decided to marry. Furthermore, the rural schools were able to fill their teaching positions with certified and well-qualified married teachers who could not be employed in the urban schools because of their policies.

WHAT THEY TAUGHT

> Then she began to plan; she would have reading, arithmetic, and grammar recitations in the forenoon, and, in the afternoon, reading again, history, writing, and spelling.
> —Laura Ingalls Wilder (*These Happy Golden Years*, 1943, 17)

Opening Exercises

The school day began with opening exercises. By Pennsylvania state law at that time, each public school session began with the Pledge of Allegiance to the flag, recitation of the Lord's Prayer, and the oral reading of ten verses from the Holy Scriptures. Subsequent Supreme Court decisions in the 1960s deemed the reading of the scripture and the oral recitation of prayer unconstitutional in order to preserve separation of church and state. But in the one-room schools the opening exercises were very important as a prelude to the school day.

Mabel Foellner told about the opening exercises in the country school in which she taught in the 1930s. "A portion of the Bible was read and we saluted the flag. I had a pitch pipe that I had brought from the teachers college at Kutztown, and we'd sing songs like 'America' and 'Columbia, the Gem of the Ocean.' We had songbooks, the old *Golden Favorites,* and we'd spend fifteen minutes singing. You might read them a story, or maybe a child came with something that he wanted to tell. It was not your 'Show and Tell' like you had later on, but maybe he had been someplace special and wanted to tell about it. You know, it was like one big family."

Kay Fox told us that her teacher, Miss Paul, used the opening as a way to literally warm up the class. "We'd have our little exercises out in the yard every morning that the weather was fit. We'd line up and make a big square in the yard. She'd bring her little square table out and have a little Victrola with a record on it. She would turn it up real loud so that we could hear it, then count one, two, three, four, and we would raise our arms above our heads, then even with our shoulders, and down to our side. We'd do that for a while; then we'd do exercises with our legs. Those of us who could stoop over and touch our toes, we would do that. Not all of them could. They were a little pudgy. Of course, I was skinny at that time so I could do it. That was physical education. We'd march around the complete yard, then around the school desks, and then we'd sit down and start our school day."

Educational theorists often make a distinction between the "formal curriculum" and the "hidden curriculum" of the school. The formal curriculum consists of the academic subjects that are taught from textbooks and courses of study, while the hidden curriculum contains the values that are transmitted by the kind of culture that the school represents. One way of making this distinction is that the formal curriculum is "taught," while the hidden curriculum is "caught." In the opening exercises the teachers taught, in the sense that specific children read the Bible and all of the children sang the favorite songs, but values were being caught at the same time.

State law required that the Bible be read and the Pledge be said. Certainly the state legislature required these exercises in the expectation that patriotism and morality would be formed by them. The rest of the opening exercises depended upon the judgment and the competence of the teacher. Miss Paul used the opening exercise as a means to develop physical skills and coordination. Miss Foellner had learned to set a key for singing with her pitch pipe and had singing as a staple in her opening exercises. Other teachers could play the piano themselves, or had older girls in the school who would play the piano to lead the singing of patriotic or old favorite songs.

Miss Foellner had an additional goal. That was to develop the speaking skills and confidence of the students by giving them a chance to make a short oral report. She used the opening exercises to develop rapport.

TEACHING THE THREE "R'S"

> The greatest single hindrance to effective use of the facilities afforded in small rural schools is the large number of subjects which divide the school day and week among them.
>
> —Fannie Wyche Dunn
> (*The Child in the Rural Environment*, 1951, 201)

After the opening exercises the serious work of teaching the academic subjects would begin. Teaching effectively in a one-room school required careful planning and recordkeeping. The teachers were expected to provide coverage in all of the conventional subject areas for all grades. The methodology of oral recitation was the technique that permeated the school day in most schools. In virtually all of the descriptions that former teachers and students provided, recitation was the major method that was used in teaching the academics. Apparently a teacher-centered classroom that stressed recitation was widespread.

Larry Cuban, a scholar and teacher at Stanford University, has completed a historical study of teaching methodology across the nation during the twentieth century. Cuban cites a study of rural schools in Pennsylvania in 1920:

In 18 Pennsylvania counties with mainly rural schools in 1920, 62% of teachers in one-room schools reported on who they were and what they did. The median age of teachers, of whom 76% were female, was 23. Most had begun teaching at age 19. Almost four out of five teachers lacked a high school diploma or any formal teacher training. Class size averaged 26 in the 18 counties, with about a quarter of the teachers reporting enrollments over 35 students. Teacher's reports of how many recitations they had—that is, how many times a day they questioned students in each grade within the class—would stagger today's teachers. One out of four teachers said they had conducted 30 or more recitations a day. The median was 26. Since the school day averaged 5.5 hours (330 minutes), apart from recess and lunch, teachers reporting 30 or more recitations met daily for at least 10 minutes with one or more students, dismissed them, met with another group, and so on. Even the State Department of Education's formal course of study recommended only 23 daily recitations. All of this suggests the hectic schedule a teacher in a one-room school followed. (Cuban, 1993, 122–23)

Teachers in southeastern Pennsylvania were generally better prepared professionally than those described in the report cited above. Later in this chapter, the types and duration of training of the teachers that we interviewed will be described. In this section we will report on the ways in which teachers managed their classes for instruction, which was predominantly the technique of a series of oral recitations, as Cuban described above. Many of those that we interviewed recalled as an advantage the type of pedagogy in which members of one class would be reciting and the others toiling away at their seat work. The classrooms were open, so students who were doing seat work would be able to turn some of their attention to the recitations.

Melvin Mack described his first two years of teaching in 1935–37. In his first year of teaching, he had fifty students; in his second he had thirty-five students. Although he was a college graduate and had had some teacher training, facing this classroom of students of diverse ages was a challenge. "In the one-room school, all fifty kids were sitting there and I really wasn't trained to teach them, because I had no course in teaching in one-room schools. I had gone to Franklin and Marshall College and had an elementary certificate, not a rural certificate. I had the college provisional certificate.

"So, the way it worked, you had to bring the first grade up front, while all the rest sat back and had busy work. You might have reading for six first-graders, and the others were working on busy work or helping others. But you had to have it all planned. A terrific amount of planning."

"Busy work" was the term used by teachers during the 1930s for what contemporary teachers might call "seat work." This would be the assigned work that the students would do in a subject so that they would be ready for the next class. There were no mimeograph machines, spirit duplicators, or photocopy machines, which teachers have used more recently to prepare seat work. The teacher usually used either the problems provided in the textbooks or wrote the assignments on the chalkboard.

Mabel Foellner, who was teaching in the 1930s, described the planning she did prior to the beginning of the school term. "I worked out a schedule. I knew which grades I was going to have. I tried to get all of the subjects in as often as I could. You had arithmetic every day. That was very important to do. I remember in arithmetic, I had one boy who just couldn't get fractions. Then he grew up to be a real estate agent. He didn't need fractions.

"English was both composition and spoken English. Teachers corrected their papers, and they weren't just true and false questions. You gave them compositions. They could write compositions in those days. Now you didn't expect a fourth-grader to do like an eighth-grader, but they learned punctuation and capitalization, and all that. I remember teaching grammar, correct usage, and the eight parts of speech.

"We had nature study. I had a class at Kutztown when I did my teacher preparation where the teacher taught us to love your surroundings. We always lived on a farm, so I tried to pass the love of nature on to my school children, too."

Miss Foellner described the evolution of her personal love of nature. "One of my own schoolteachers was from Doylestown. She taught us the love of wildflowers. People didn't have mowed lawns like they do today. Wildflowers were plentiful, so we learned the names of the wildflowers. She would have a wildflower contest. One boy would always win it. He lived back in the woods, in a swampy area, and the flowers would always open early for him. So he got the prize for bringing in the most wild flowers."

Kay Fox recalled that the older students were sometimes permitted to assist the teacher. "While one class was reciting the others had to be studying and keep very, very quiet. The older ones, as we knew our lessons real well, on a Friday were allowed to stand in the back of the school to help teach the first or second grades, while Miss Paul was teaching the third, fourth, and fifth grades. That was supposed to be a help to her, and we were really proud to do it because we were playing teacher."

Emma Weirbach recalled the techniques that Mr. Frankenfield used in her school about 1910. Penmanship by the Palmer Method of writing was an important subject, especially for the younger students. "When the day started we had Bible reading; the teacher read. Then we had a prayer, then we sang, not just hymns. We sang a lot, songs like 'America' and Christmas songs. We'd start the day with penmanship. We had penmanship a couple of times a week, when you made the ovals and everything. He taught us you move your whole hand, not just your fingers. And we had up-downs to do.

"Then the three Rs, spelling, geography, and physiology, which they called health. You wouldn't have them every day, because there were eight grades. Certain things on certain days. For the beginners, as soon as they learned their first letter that he'd put on the blackboard, then they got their first book. When he was teaching the little ones, we others were doing our lessons."

Instruction in penmanship using ink was recalled by many of the older individuals. They did not have ballpoint, or even fountain pens, but straight pens that had to be dipped into an inkwell that was placed in a hole in the desktop. There was a small reservoir for ink in the pen point itself, but the pen point had to be dipped often into the inkwell. These pens could leave big blots, so they were not used by the younger students until their fine motor coordination was developed. A mystique grew up about the opportunity for boys to be mischievous by dipping into the inkwell the pigtails of the girls sitting in the desk in front of them.

Florence Vogt remembered using ink pens. "We had those old inkwell things, dip pens, but we younger ones didn't use them until later on. There was always some smart-aleck kids who would dip the pen in and throw the ink. We learned to write with ink about the fourth or fifth grade."

Marian Stumb Renninger also recalled students getting into mischief with ink pens. "We had little inkwells in the upper right-hand corner of our desks. It was horrible for a child to get used to those pens, because you had to hold them just a certain way to make them write decent. I remember that the girls who wore braids had to be careful that the boys didn't stick them down in the inkwell."

Clara Willauer Kipp described the ways in which schooling was made interesting. "One of the good things that I think was meaningful to me as a child was to watch the older ones do math on the board or do other work. You just couldn't wait until you got that far so you could do it, too.

"We had contests in geography, where we were lined up on each side. And then we had contests in math working on the board. The teacher would give you a column to add for speed. It was fun for the younger ones to watch that. It gave them an incentive to learn and progress.

"We had no science. It was reading, writing, arithmetic, and geography. There was a great deal of memorization—like the various state capitals. We had to memorize the activities of the various presidents, the accomplishments of that president. Like you'd take the 'M' in Madison and think of something he did, like 'management.'

"There was an emphasis on grammar and correct usage, parts of speech, and parsing. We loved that. I guess everything fascinated me. The parsing of English was very helpful in learning Latin when I went to high school and college.

"The teachers would have their hands full teaching the basics, when you had that many children. The older students would often times take the younger students to hear their reading lessons or their spelling words. The teacher would assign them.

"We learned to write with pen and ink. We had little glass inkwells in our desks. We were always delighted when we got old enough to use those pens. We had penmanship—the Palmer Method. We made circles and copied samples of letters."

As was reported in the story of Ruth Hackman in Chapter 2, her teachers had brought samples of penmanship exercises that had been done by students in the coal regions in Pennsylvania that approached being works of art. They were done by the typical way of teaching penmanship, the Palmer Method.

Prior to the 1930s, the rural schoolchildren had individual slates to work math problems. One purpose of using slates was to save paper, which was expensive. Clara Willauer Kipp recalled using slates for seat work as Carrie Frankenfield Horne had in her story. "I remember we had slates. To keep us busy you had little sticks, thicker than match sticks, to make patterns out of them. The slates were about eight inches by ten inches. I suppose the school gave them to us. We must have left them in the school when we went home at night."

The "sticks" that she mentioned probably were a type of hard chalk, or slate pencil, that was used to write on the slates.

Teaching was very textbook centered in the basics, such as mathematics. If the textbook did not explain a math problem adequately, that could cause difficulty for the teacher and the students. Ed Fox recalled a difficult math problem. "In the arithmetic book on page 110, in the sixth or seventh grade, there was a problem. There was a diagram of a property. The dimensions of the property were given and I think we were supposed to figure out how many acres were involved. It was a stickler for every class. Every class had trouble with the problem on page 110. I can remember so well. I can still almost visualize the shape of the diagram. Strange, but that was a stickler for every class that came along, the problem on page 110."

Teachers used other techniques beside recitation and seat work. Rochelle Renninger Boyle recalled a technique one of her teachers used to make learning more fun when she was a student at Scholl's School. "There were times that we all got a chance to participate. One story that we studied was like a play—something with the 'Golden Goose.' Our teacher, Mrs. Esther Kurtz, had this old stuffed pheasant. That was the 'golden goose,' and whoever touched the golden goose got stuck to it. And so you'd end up with a whole column of people. Almost everybody in the class would end up being stuck to the golden goose, and we would be walking all around the classroom, everybody stuck to each other."

The schools had few audio-visual resources, but Mary Strock recalled the use of the radio for enrichment in her one-room school in the 1930s.

"We used the Columbia School of the Air. I had a radio in that room. I had sent in a subscription and I got information about what was going to be taught in music, what was going to be taught in math. Sometimes we would listen to that if we had gotten all our work done. That was quite an innovation at that time. It came out of New York. I had a teacher's guide. It was mostly music and art, as I remember."

By the 1930s, scholars in rural education were advocating the clustering of groups of students to create instructional groups in which there were more than just one or two students. There was some evidence that this type of grouping was practiced in the schools that our interviewees attended. Perhaps the most typical was the acceleration of bright pupils through the curriculum.

Grace Knapp provides an example of such grouping. "There were only two of us in sixth grade and two of us in seventh grade, so the teacher had us together. The two of us in the seventh grade were able to take the eighth-grade tests and we were permitted to go to high school. So that's how I got to high school earlier, in seven years."

Mary Strock also completed elementary school early by acceleration. "I did seventh and eighth grade in one year. In a one-room school, it really didn't matter if you skipped a grade. You see, you paid attention to what was being taught if it was your grade or not, so they could put children ahead then if the child had a little ambition. They could do all the work in less time because it was available. You could listen to all the grade levels."

Conversely, teachers could hold students back if they were progressing less rapidly, or if it were the opinion of the teacher that more development or instruction was necessary before the students were ready for high school, as was discussed in the interview with Ruth Hackman.

The task of planning for teaching and the sheer load of paperwork in grading papers and preparing materials were daunting. However, two former teachers told how teachers worked together, even though they taught in separate isolated schools. Sharing of test-making was one example. Mary Strock told how she and another teacher in rural Springfield Township shared tests.

"When I was teaching in one school, and Margaret Seylar in another school, along with other teachers, we would exchange tests. Maybe this marking period I would make the math test, Margaret would make the history test, somebody would make the reading test. We coordinated our teaching effort, way back then. Now they don't even do that."

In many school districts, teachers were required to attend school board meetings. They received their monthly pay personally when they submitted their registers (reports on the attendance of students). Anna Neamand, a teacher in Richland Township, tells how the teachers used this time efficiently. "The board meetings were different than they are today. We teachers were required to attend. We had to be there at eight o'clock to pick up our supplies of the month. The board went into session, and we had to wait until they finished and adjourned before we dare have our checks for the month. So we got them at midnight.

"But in between, the teachers sat in the corner in the back and compared teaching assignments, courses and curriculum, and course of study. We made uniform tests for our students, so at each school instruction would develop along the same lines. Then one teacher was in charge of tests in geography, another in history. Then we'd rotate the tasks. We'd make the tests for the next month and supply them among the schools. There was work done at these meetings, even though we sat and waited for a check."

Commentary

What emerges from an examination of the discussion by the former students and teachers is an image of a schoolroom that stressed the basics as they were generally taught in the first half of the twentieth century. There was a solid grounding in the traditional academics, the "three Rs" of reading, 'riting, and 'rithmetic, augmented by history, geography, spelling, and health, or physiology and sometimes nature study.

Generally, teachers taught by and from the book. The textbooks were of sturdy construction, as they had to last a long time, and there was not the concept of knowledge changing rapidly as an excuse for changing textbooks every few years. Then, as now, the textbook is the most prevalent instructional aid that most teachers have.

Teachers taught "from" the book for many reasons. The textbooks were considered to be authoritative, and the conventional image of the teacher was of respect for the teacher as an authoritative figure. If the teachers did not have a teacher's edition of the math textbook, which had the correct answers, they were prudent enough to work the problems in advance and to pencil in the correct answers before recitation. The textbooks contained the information that would be tested in the eighth-grade examination. And the textbooks often included problems or assignments of exercises that could be assigned as seat work that would keep the students occupied between recitations. Educational theorists were beginning to advocate more of an activity-based classroom as early as the 1920s, even for the rural schools, but the reality was that a textbook-based curriculum was probably the most practical for the rural schools.

Teachers taught "by" the book as well. Recitation was the most ordinary form of instruction. At the end of each recitation the teacher would make an assignment for the next recitation. As was noted previously, this environment, in which oral recitation was going on much of the time, had its advantages. Most of those that we interviewed had been good students, and they typically had been able to "tune in" on the lessons that other classes were reciting even while they were working on their own seat work. In effect, a student was an auditor and spectator each year of the whole eight-year curriculum, while a participant in the curriculum of just one grade level per year. The former students who were reflective about this as a preview and review of the lessons that they studied saw repetition as an advantage. The teachers often used the oral recitation to their advantage, as well, for they could accelerate or decelerate the pace of students through the instructional program, depending upon their ability.

Elementary classrooms today have a great variety of instructional technologies. In the post–World War II period several communications technologies that had been perfected during the war became adapted for the classroom. Elementary teachers today have available to them computers, video technologies, overhead projectors, motion picture projectors, and other devices that weren't even dreamed of in the one-room school. But neither did most of the urban schools have much in the way of technologies other than slide picture projectors and record players. A few teachers had radios in the classrooms, and programs such as the Columbia School of the Air were utilized by enterprising teachers such as Mary Strock. In the early decade of the century each child would have a personal slate to calculate math at his or her desk, but the small slates seem to have disappeared by the 1920s. The large slate blackboards had been installed behind the teacher's desks a long time ago, and they were permanent. They lasted as long as the one-room schools. The slate boards are still there in schools that are used as museums.

It is accurate to say that the teachers in the one-room school emphasized the three "Rs." They taught the traditional academic three "Rs" as basic tool subjects, but the curriculum was taught by procedures that could also be called the three "Rs": "recitation," "repetition," and "reinforcement." But the routines of recitation could be spiced by innovative techniques, such as "trapping," or academic competition within a grade level class. Repetition permitted the teachers some flexibility in the tempo in which the curriculum was covered by individual students, particularly the faster and slower students. Virtually all of the former students felt that their learning had been reinforced by the method of oral recitations that characterized the one-room school methodology. For the students, there was an important "fourth R" or recess, but that will be described in the next chapter.

LITERARY PROGRAMS

As a way to end the week on a pleasant note, many one-room schools used the final hour or so of class time on Friday afternoon for a literary program. These programs were performances by the students. There were opportunities to sing, recite poems, or to take part in academic contests, or "bees."

Mabel Foellner recalled the literary programs. "In my elementary days, on one Friday afternoon a month, for about an hour, we'd have what was called a 'literary program.' Some who liked to sing, might sing. Some would recite. When I taught, each child was to memorize one poem a month. You gave them a choice. For each month of the school year, there was a list of poems the first graders were to choose from."

And Mary Weikel recalled the literary program on a Friday afternoon as, "our best day. In the afternoon we'd sing, or recite poetry. I still remember some of it. Some time ago I was reciting some poetry to a friend. She had never heard of it. [Mary Weikel recited the first verse of 'September.'] We learned a verse a week."

Thus she could recall and recite the first verse from the poem, although it had been at least seventy years since she had been required to memorize it.

Sometimes the program was not very literary. Glenn Haring recalled a Friday afternoon "literary program." "Every Friday afternoon we had a literary. Then we'd have wrestling matches up on the platform. This one fellow, my opponent that I was going to wrestle, weighed about one hundred pounds more than I did. The teacher was the referee. The rules were that if one person gave up, the other one won. Well, this fellow had me down on the floor, and I took my thumb and I pushed his nose in as hard as I could push it, and he gave up [chuckle]. Whatever you did to make the other fellow give up, you were the winner. I can remember that as if it were yesterday."

DISCIPLINE

The type, degree and effectiveness of discipline seemed to vary with the personalities of the teacher and the general deportment of the students. Acceptable behavior was very important. As Ruth Hackman had reported earlier, students in her school received a grade in deportment. A grade of a "C" was cause for alarm in her family.

Particularly in the early years covered by our study, corporal punishment was an acceptable treatment for misbehavior. Probably the threat of corporal punishment was a necessary survival technique of many teachers. Generally, the use of corporal punishment was accepted in the homes of the students. The conventional wisdom was that if a child was punished in school, he would also be punished when he went home. We had almost no reports of corporal punishment of female students.

Teachers and students reported many milder forms of punishment, such as being required to stay in school during recess or after school or to write compositions or to copy lessons or to sit or stand in a designated spot. In some cases assignment of chores in the school seemed to be used as a punishment, in other cases assignment of a student to do chores was seen as a reward, as will be reported in the next chapter. The stories varied tremendously about the discipline techniques of the teachers.

Emma Weirbach was a student during World War I. She spoke of the support that the family was expected to give to the teacher when children were disciplined in school. Her teacher must have figuratively had eyes in the back of his head. "We had a very strict teacher, and when he was writing on the blackboard and you were back at your seat and talking, the keys came right over his shoulder and came right back near where you were talkin'. He never looked. He just throwed [*sic*] them right back over his shoulder. He knew who it was. Then you'd bring the keys up to him and then maybe you stood in the corner for a while.

"That's the punishment we got, but we never had much of it because he was firm and what he said counted. The children respected and liked him. I don't think the children were that bad because they were brought up by their parents and family at home that they were to listen, because my father always said, 'If you ever get punished in school, you'll get a worse one when you come home.' My father was strict."

The teacher, Mr. Frankenfield [the brother of Carrie Frankenfield Horne], apparently also knew how to head off possible discipline problems. Emma Weirbach continued the story. "He was a wonderful teacher. He had a system and we abided by it. So if we got a little noisy, like you did especially on a rainy day, he said, 'Everybody stop, get up, raise the windows on both sides,' and we took exercise. 'One, two, three, four.' After we did that maybe ten minutes, 'Sit down now and get back to work.'

"I never saw him whip anyone. One time my brother had licked a bigger fellow who was always making fun of our father, so my brother that next day put two pairs of pants on. That day the teacher called them both up on the platform, made them shake hands, and say they were sorry. He said, 'I want you to be friends. I don't want to hear any more about this.' From that time on that boy never bothered my brother. If there was any serious fighting, that's the way the teacher solved it."

The students in Tohickon School had a reputation for misbehavior, and the teacher responded with harsher discipline and corporal punishment. Woodrow Barringer told this story about student behavior and discipline in his school in the 1920. "At that time we had on the average fifty-two pupils with one teacher. Nix-nutsy bunch of pupils you don't find very often, is what we were. [Nix-nutsy was Pennsylvania German slang for those who misbehaved.] The teacher caught me throwing notes across the aisle to one of the girls, and after a while he got tired of it and said, 'You pack your books and get over there and sit with her in the double seat and then you don't have to do that.' She was a wild one. We read more true stories and modern romance than we done [sic] anything else. Geography books were just about the right size to hide them. We would share the same magazines. Every now and then he would catch us reading them. He would go down to the heater and throw the magazine in.

"That teacher had eyes in the back of his head. You didn't pull nothing [sic] on that man. When he first came there, he had boys who were at least eight inches taller than he was, and he was an average tall man. One day he caught two of them doing something they weren't supposed to, I can't remember what, and he made them stand up there on the platform. This happened right after recess, and the one guy was going to take a poke at him. Well, the teacher had a hickory stick about thirty inches long, and almost a half inch thick. And he came down on that kid's arm so that it cracked. He said, 'There's nobody going to take a poke at me, my pupils or anybody else, and from this day on all of you remember that.' That kid had a black and blue mark on his arm for a couple of months. The boy would have been sixteen or seventeen. It was his last year of school, eighth grade.

"The teacher was a bald-headed man, not a hair on his head. Some of the boys would make spit balls and had these little willow sticks, hollowed out, and they'd blow spit balls at his bald head when he had his head turned. Well, that went on for a couple of months. One day he turned around and rapped that stick across his desk. There was nobody in their seats, all out of their seats. Boy, he come [sic] down. 'If there's any more of that I'll make a thorough search, one by one, and when I find the one who has them [sic] blow-guns he'll wish he never had 'em [sic].' Well, that quit that. The kids didn't dislike the teacher. It was only devilment, that's all."

William Steers had attended a two-room school near Haddonfield, New Jersey during World War I. He discussed the discipline techniques of one of his female teachers. "Mrs. Barton was a very patient woman, but she used to beat the hell out of us. She would say, 'Go cut a switch.' So you would go outside and try to cut a switch that wouldn't hurt you too much. Then she would switch us on the seat. If I told my mother, I got another beatin' for being bad. So I wouldn't tell.

"The teacher would just switch you a couple of times, not a real beating. She was very nice. She'd do it for things like sassing her back or not doing our lesson. Or we'd get switched for dipping the girls' hair in the inkwells. We did that. The boys sat separated from the girls, and if you were bad you had to sit with the girls. We hated that.

"When I was in the early grades the teacher didn't use a switch, just stand us in the corner. I hated that. Put a dunce cap on you, sit you on a high stool, keep your back to the class. If you did anything too bad they kept you in for recess, not after school."

Mr. Steers was the only former student who reported wearing a dunce cap. That does not seem to be a prevalent practice in the twentieth-century rural school.

Frank Speer attended a one-room school near Doylestown, in Bucks County, in the 1930s. He reported that he had a teacher with just one arm, but she nevertheless practiced corporal punishment. "She was a strict disciplinarian. She had her favorite way of treating transgressors. I really know well, because I was an 'A' student in everything but deportment. I guess I was bored, because everything was easy for me. I was always writing notes and pulling girls' hair, and things like that, which little boys are prone to do. Girls had long hair in those days. So whenever I was caught, I was given a pen knife and I went out to the hedge fence and cut switches. Now, depending upon the crime you cut anywhere from one to ten switches, and she broke the switches on you. She would use ten switches on you if the crime was that bad. She really didn't hurt you that much, because the switches were thin, and I used to cut little notches in them so they'd break easy."

Martha Tarantino remembered corporal punishment by a teacher in her school. "He had a nice wide board. He didn't hit them on the legs; he hit them on the seat. He'd make them bend over the seat in front of all the others. If they did something on the playground they shouldn't, they got it right when they came in the door. He'd stand there and crack 'em one. I think they deserved it. They were rowdies. No kid ever fought the teacher. Afterward the teacher told me, 'You know, I've wondered if after these boys get older what they would do to me.' But he said they all treated him nice."

Robert Tarantino had a number of teachers in his school in the period just before World War I, several of whom used corporal punishment. But he noted that they varied in their personalities, and this influenced the techniques that they used. "There were a couple of teachers that never used any punishment. Frank Hartman was one; later he became an insurance man. He had something about him that people just listened. It's marvelous how some can handle people."

Marian Stumb Renninger told us about the influence of the personality of one of her teachers. "Something that I remember most about her is that she never raised her voice. The teacher never raised her voice no matter what anybody did; she would be calm and collected. But she would talk to them; make them know they had done wrong. She was able to keep good discipline.

"I had to stand in the corner one time for talking when I shouldn't have. I had to face the blackboard for a good hour, I'd say. I never remember any teacher slapping anyone or anything like that. No paddling, but they'd get a hold of the students' shoulders and shake them."

Many times there were several children from the same family in the same school. They monitored the behavior of their siblings and sometimes they stuck up for their brothers or sisters. Glenn Haring told this story about a large family and the way they interacted in school when a sibling was being disciplined. "This family had a lot of children, like twelve or thirteen, so you had a lot of brothers and sisters in the same school. When this teacher was going to spank a first-grader her older sister got the teacher by the throat and was choking her, to protect her little sister. Then one of the eighth-grade boys got ahold [sic] of the girl who was choking the teacher and twisted her arm until she let go. The teacher, you see, was there all by herself. She had no principal to go to. And there were sometimes forty-five to fifty kids."

If corporal punishment was considered necessary, the smaller teacher was at a disadvantage, especially if the students were overage. Glenn Haring told this story about a tiny teacher and a big boy.

"We had a lot of big children because some of them didn't start school until they were eight, so they'd be like sixteen in the eighth grade. From eighth grade they'd go right into the farm or the factory. A lot of the girls went into the factory, also.

"I don't remember what this kid did. Mrs. K. was such a small lady, very little. She pulled this fellow out of his seat and she jumped on top of him with her feet, up on top of him, and he just giggled the whole time. He was on the floor, laughing at her. When it was all over she sent him home."

Apparently many or even most teachers did not have to resort to spanking the students. Mary Dietz had been both a student and a teacher in one-room schools. We asked her about the need for punishment of students in the one-room schools. "Very few were punished because there was no need. I think the discipline at home has disappeared today. Here is a nice story on that: At the end of the year I had to collect the birth certificates of each child in the first grade, and I found out that I had been misspelling the name of a little Polish boy all year. His mother had told him to tell me to get it corrected, but he told her, 'Oh, no, you told me the teacher is always right.'

"One thing I found that if you are strict with your students right away and let them know you are the teacher and you are to teach them; you are not really there to discipline them, be a constable or something like that. You were the teacher to teach."

Harold Koder was a teacher while he was still in his teens. He told of the discipline techniques that he used. "Our usual discipline technique was to have them stand in the corner, or we used to take recess privileges away from them. Or we'd give them something to do. One of the things that I did most, if I had a pupil, boy or girl, who had done something that I had told them they were not allowed to do and if they repeated it, I'd get their history book, or whatever their weak subject was, I'd get that out, and I'd say, 'Now here's something that I want you to do. I want you to spend every recess until further notice, copying this chapter.' That way, I was taking their recess privileges, and they didn't have to sit in their seats and scowl and make a face. But they were doing something that was helping them in the subject they were weak in."

Perhaps the most humane story about student discipline was told by Kay Fox, whose favorite teacher was Miss Paul. Male students sat on one side of the room, while female students sat on the other, though that practice seems to have disappeared by the mid-1930s. "If we did something that we weren't allowed to do, talk back to the teacher, didn't know our lesson, she would punish us by sitting us with a boy across the room. The boys sat on one side of the school room and we girls sat on the other, two to a desk. And we would have to sit with a boy that we definitely did not like. That was punishment.

"Then, another thing we would do, a tricky thing we would do. The pencil sharpener was on the other side of the room, the boys' side. So we would intentionally break the point of the pencil so that we could march around the back of the room so that we could go over and sharpen them.

"Then we would slip the boys notes that we would see them after school on the corner of the porch and find out what they were going to bring for lunch the next day. If the teacher didn't see us, we'd swap apples or candy or something in our lunch. We thought that was a big deal too.

"There again, if we did something tricky or something we weren't supposed to do, we would be punished by having to clean up the books, and do the erasers, and sweep the floors, and things like that. So that was just part of our punishment.

"Miss Paul never spanked children. No, her punishment was to have you stay after school or to take recess away, or you sit with a boy you don't like. The kids would giggle, you know. Things like that."

Commentary

In America, schools and teachers stand *in loco parentis*, in the place of the parents. During the first half of the twentieth century corporal punishment was acceptable, if it was considered necessary by either parents or teachers. But there were many cases reported where corporal punishment was never administered in individual schools. In other cases, the persons who were punished reported it matter-of-factly, often while remarking about how "nice" the teacher was.

Perhaps a teacher like Miss Paul was the norm, by the latter part of the era of the one-room school. The students would find ways to challenge the authority of the teacher, but she would use a variety and range of management and human relations skills to maintain order.

From approximately 1900 until about 1925, the early part of the period that we studied, very young persons could become teachers, sometimes while still in their teens. They had little training in classroom management. There was a very tenuous support system behind them. There were no school principals in the country schools. School boards would generally "back" a teacher, but the teacher had to confess that he or she could not handle the situation in order to bring it to the attention of the school board. Some teachers resorted to corporal punishment in order to survive.

TEACHER PREPARATION

> A teacher has many beginnings. His first experience is usually had when he begins the induction process into practice teaching in a normal school or a state teachers college. He will begin again after he is licensed by a state accrediting agency and assumes the full responsibility of teaching a group of children. The second experience will have in it many elements of the practice teaching but it will have new ones also, for it will be without supervision, and the teacher must rely on himself.
> —Kate V. Wofford (*Teaching in Small Schools*, 1946, 4)

In order to be employed in the public schools, an individual had to be certified. Several individuals who had been teachers detailed their certification programs. Two of those who began teaching in the 1920s were employed without professional study beyond high school other than summer school work at a nearby college.

Harold Koder taught for a few years in the early 1920s. He took summer school courses at Muhlenberg College, most after he had started to teach, in order to qualify for a teaching certificate.

"The first year that I taught was 1922. I graduated from high school in 1920 at the age of sixteen. I was too young to teach school and I thought I wanted to, so I got a job in a grocery store for several years. During that time I went to Muhlenberg College and took up some summer school courses that they recommended. In addition to the teaching school diploma, we had to have a few credits and then were able to teach.

"I took summer work for the four years that I was teaching. Here are the subjects that I studied at Muhlenberg: In my first year, 1922, the first subject was physiology and hygiene. The second one was oral and silent reading. The third was elementary education. The fourth was music. Those were the four subjects that I took during the summer from July 3 to August 11 of 1922.

"The second summer, 1923, I took geography, the teaching of English, hygiene, and penmanship. In the third year, 1924, I studied school art, arithmetic, educational administration, and introduction to teaching. I don't know why I didn't get that the first year. During the fourth year I had zoology, zoology laboratory work, German, and history of education. I took summer work for the four years that I was teaching.

"I ended up with what they called a partial certificate. I received a letter that was dated February 3, 1923, that evaluated my credits. It told me that I needed sixty-two additional semester hours of professional credits in order to qualify for the standard certificate. I would have had to have sixty-two credits by 1927. I would have had to go to school at a state teachers' college or Muhlenberg College. So I never completed the standard certificate. But I had had the experience of being a student in a one-room school. I knew what had to be done.

"When I got enough credits to begin, in 1922, when I became eighteen, I taught school in the Tohickon School, which was in Richland Township. My pay was seventy-five dollars per school month. Six hundred dollars a year. No fringe benefits. And build the fires and clean the building and teach."

Mr. Koder taught in four different schools over the next four years, then gave up teaching for work in the post office. Given the lack of tenure, no year-to-year contracts, and extensive further course requirements, one can understand Mr. Koder's decision to try a career other than teaching. He began in the Tohickon School with thirty-seven students; then was given a school with fifty students. He taught in a different school each year. As he remarked, "I was looking ahead. I was trying to find an occupation that provided more security than school teaching did then. They didn't have a tenure system at that time."

Just as men who were the breadwinners needed to have an opportunity for steady wages, women needed a profession where they could combine a professional life with a conventional family life. Mary Hager Dietz was able to pursue a teaching career, raise a family, and return to teaching when the family was grown. She taught in the Rocky Ridge School from 1927–29, then returned to teaching in 1944 in the same school. "Teaching was my choice from the very day I started to go to school. My mother had been a teacher. After high school I wanted to go to college but my boyfriend said, 'I'm afraid you'll forget me if you go to college.' I said, 'All right, I won't go to college. I'll get my college education along the way.' And I did. I went to Muhlenberg during summer times. We were allowed to take courses at Muhlenberg. It was a college where many who wanted to become teachers could go and get certification.

"I started teaching right out of high school. I was supposed to go to college and earn some credits. It took at least ten years until I got the teaching certificate. I taught two years, then got married, and we moved to Philadelphia. I married the boy who kept me from going to college. Then in 1944 I went back to teaching, in the same school where I had started teaching, the Rocky Ridge School.

"When I got out of high school I was only seventeen and I applied to the Richland School Board. I didn't realize you couldn't teach until you were eighteen. So I applied and got the job at Rocky Ridge. I was so happy; I was in heaven. And I worked so hard up at Muhlenburg to take as many courses as I could in the summertime. Then one day one of the members of the school board came to see me and said, 'You know, we just found out that you are only seventeen and you can't teach until eighteen.' I only missed it by one month, so I wasn't too heartbroken. Then they told me, 'You have to get a substitute teacher.' 'Oh,' I thought, 'a substitute teacher. I've never done this before. What am I going to do?'

"So I thought of a friend of mine who had been a teacher, Mrs. Leroy Strunk. Then she got married, too, and had a little boy. She agreed to substitute for me. It was a matter of six weeks. The school board had said, 'The day you become eighteen you can go over there and be the teacher. You have that school assigned to you and we are not going to take it from you.'

"But while Mrs. Strunk substituted for me I had to hook my horse up in the morning, take the carriage, put up the little folding top, and go out and pick Mrs. Strunk up, and take her out to Paletown Road and let her off at the school. Then I came home, unhooked my horse, put him in the stable again, and then in the afternoon I did the same thing. I enjoyed taking her out and getting her.

"Organizing the school day came naturally. We had done that when I was a student in the country school. We were very well acquainted with the procedures. We had our little ones first and then in the afternoon the youngest had plenty of time to rest. Some would fall asleep, and that was all right. Some of them sat and listened when you taught the upper grades and that helped them so much. You would be surprised how much they learned from hearing the others. When you were in the second grade and you knew what the fifth- and sixth-graders were doing, that helped a lot.

"Up at Muhlenberg we had a class in procedures. All the courses I took those first two summers at Muhlenberg were very good. We had a very good woman as reading teacher. She gave me an outline that gave me a very good idea of what should be taught in reading, and I followed her advice. Then we had an ornithology course, and I just loved that course. The professor had bird models and you had to go around and identify every one, one hundred birds, and I got them all right, every one."

Mary Dietz returned to teaching during World War II. She continued her education on a part-time basis. When the country schools were consolidated, she moved into the consolidated school and completed her career there.

There were other routes into teaching. In an earlier chapter, Carrie Frankenfield Horne and Mamie Fluck Kratzer described their two-year programs at Kutztown State Normal School, which became Kutztown State Teachers College in 1927, when prospective teachers could earn a bachelor's degree in education as well as a teaching certificate.

Melvin Mack had graduated from Franklin and Marshall College in the 1930s, during the Great Depression. Employment of any kind was difficult. Mr. Mack decided to prepare to be a teacher after he had completed his bachelor's degree.

"After I graduated from college I got no teaching certificate. I wanted to be an actuary, a statistician. I majored in math and statistics at Franklin and Marshall. I graduated during the 1930s. I went to New York to the insurance companies and I couldn't find anything. This was in 1934.

"I happened to get a job with a county superintendent doing some national security work. This was during the Depression, one of the alphabet organizations of the New Deal. I told the county superintendent, 'I'd like to be a teacher. What do I do?' He said, 'Go to Muhlenberg. Isaac Miles Wright is a big name up there in Allentown, and he is a school director on the Allentown School Board.' Mr.

Wright said, 'Sure, I can get you a certificate in less than a year in both elementary and secondary.

"I then went to Stanley Kurtz, who was the Supervising principal of Perkiomen Valley. He was my old principal of my high school. And he said, 'Yes, you can do your practice teaching here.' So I got my certificate in one year to teach elementary and secondary. I practice taught in secondary in East Greenville High School and in Green Lane I did my elementary practice teaching. I think I had to take thirty semester hours at Muhlenberg. Of course, I wasn't working and I went one year and one summer."

Melvin Mack found a teaching position in a one-room school. He then taught in high schools and became a high school principal and the supervising principal of rural Springfield Township in Bucks County. He was the founder of the Palisades School District, a consolidated school system, which provides a kindergarten through twelfth-grade education in several rural townships. He ended his professional educational career as an assistant county school superintendent in Bucks County. He explained the process for permanent certification after a person began teaching on a temporary certificate.

"You had to be rated twice a year, by state law. There was a yellow form or a checklist that had to be sent in to the county superintendent and then approved by him and sent to the state, until you had your college permanent certificate. So the first two years you worked you got evaluated twice a year. They would rate you 'satisfactory' or 'unsatisfactory.' If you were rated unsatisfactory, then of course you weren't put on tenure. That was the main objective. If rated unsatisfactory you could still continue to teach unless you got another unsatisfactory rating. If you were rated unsatisfactory after you got tenure it had to be proven. Very seldom were tenured teachers dismissed because of unsatisfactory ratings. The administrators had to have all kinds of evidence. Originally the rating of teachers was handled by the county superintendent's office, but when we became consolidated it became a local district matter for the supervising principal, who was working under the county superintendent."

Summary

There were multiple routes to a teaching certificate, as we have seen. Some teachers, like Mary Hager Dietz, Harold Koder, and Erwinna Price, who was mentioned by James Gerhart, were able to go almost directly from high school into a teaching position in a one-room school classroom. They then had the task of going for several years of summer sessions at a teacher-training institution, such as Muhlenberg College, in order to earn the credits for a permanent certificate.

The great majority of one-room school teachers, particularly after the state normal schools became teachers colleges in 1927, were prepared in the way that Carrie Frankenfield Horne, Mamie Fluck Kratzer, and Mabel Foellner became certified. They attended a normal school or state teachers college for two or more years, then were eligible to begin teaching by earning a provisional normal teaching certificate. If they taught successfully for two years, their provisional certificate was made permanent. Melvin Mack was something of an exception to the general practice, as he took his certification work in a post-baccalaureate program. The fact that he already had a bachelor's degree served him well, as this

Normal School certificate. This is a reduction of Carrie Frankenfield Horne's teaching certificate. The original is 16 × 21 inches. This certificate authorized her to teach thirty-seven different subjects for elementary school through the eighth grade. Certificate reproduced courtesy of her daughter, Mrs. Robert Heiland.

made it possible to become a high school principal and supervising principal. For those positions he needed administrative certification and at least a bachelor's degree.

Once an individual had permanent certification, no further college course work was required of Pennsylvania schoolteachers, although many teachers took courses to keep up-to-date. But a program had been developed, which was widespread in both urban and rural education, to provide on-going, noncredit experiences for practicing teachers to keep them motivated and current with new ideas. This was the teachers institute.

TEACHERS' INSTITUTES

Compared to the preparation of teachers late in the twentieth century, the typical rural schoolteacher had a minimal formal preparation. But there was a way for teachers to keep up-to-date, a very important type of continuing education. It was through "teachers institutes."

In Bucks County early in the twentieth century there was a county teachers institute held at the county seat of Doylestown. The timing was such that the county institute coincided with the fall harvest, especially the husking of corn, when the labor of schoolchildren was very much needed. Many rural school districts were sympathetic to the needs of farmers and did not invoke compulsory education rules until after the close of the teachers institute. Thus, if children were needed on the farm in September, October, and early November, the children could work at home without being troubled by truant officers.

The date of the teacher institute was vivid for Mabel Foellner, who had two uncles serving in the armed services during World War I. This was before there were radios, and telephones were still scarce. "I was ten years old in 1918. Bucks County teachers had one week of institute. During that week, we kids would help husk corn. Nearly everybody when I was in elementary school was a farmer. The corn was all husked by hand.

"I remember we were husking corn. There had been talk that things might be coming to a close in the war. Around eleven o'clock we heard the whistle blow. There were mills in Milford, New Jersey, and you could hear those. We knew then that something important must have happened. I can remember that it was the eleventh day of the eleventh month of 1918. My uncles, brothers of my mother, had enlisted, and they were coming home. I couldn't understand why those boys didn't come home from the service in a day or two."

After completion of high school, Miss Foellner prepared to teach by attending the normal school at Kutztown, at the teachers college. She then returned to her native Nockamixon Township as a rural school teacher. This provided an opportunity to attend the Bucks County teachers institute.

"County institutes were held at Doylestown, at the county seat. They were held for one week in the court room. We'd have speakers. One speaker I remember was Pearl Buck. She always wore a hat. She had come back from China, and she was telling of her experiences. They would have musical programs, or maybe a lecture. In the evening, that was more of an entertainment.

"During the day we had a lot of things that were helpful, people who would come and tell us of their experiences in teaching. That was your way of improving yourself. Later the county institutes were discontinued. Then for a while they were by regions in the county. Still later we went to Schoolman's Week, in Philadelphia. It was supposed to be helpful, but a lot of teachers went shopping. There wasn't an efficient system of checkup. If you wanted to you could get a lot of help, because there were specific programs in the classrooms of the University of Pennsylvania. In the 1960s the Schoolman's Week, which was a giant teachers institute, was discontinued."

Local School Board Institutes

Miss Foellner told about the local institutes held with the school directors. Her experience was very positive. "Local institutes were once a month, generally on the Friday nearest to the end of the month. School would close an hour early. Then we would meet with the school directors. Most of them were farmers, who could take off a couple hours. We would meet at Revere, which was sort of the center of the township.

"We would get our paycheck, then they would ask you, 'Now, are you having a problem? We're all here. Maybe we can help you, or some teacher who has taught longer than you can help you; or maybe you have a new idea that will help an older teacher.' It was a time for help. It wasn't a time for criticism. If they thought there was something they should tell you about they came to you privately at another time.

"There was a director who was given charge over each school. He sort of kept in touch. The school director would visit the school. We also had visits from the county superintendent and his assistant superintendent. The assistant superintendent was Mr. Albert Rutter. He was such a kind man, and helpful. Maybe once a year the county superintendent, Mr. J. H. Hoffman, would come and visit."

SUPERVISION AND HIRING OF TEACHERS

Prior to school consolidation, supervision of teachers in rural schools was a joint responsibility. The school board was composed of five members, who were elected as directors by the township voters.

The directors hired the teachers, purchased instructional materials, set the taxes, and saw that the school buildings were maintained. Generally they divided up responsibility for oversight of the various individual schools. They would troubleshoot and be advocates for the school (Leight, 1984; 1990).

The office of the county superintendent provided professional support for the school board members. All of the records that were required by the state were summarized and coordinated by the county superintendent's office, such as the registers that documented pupil attendance. The certification of teachers who were employed by the rural schools was handled by the county superintendent. The assistant superintendent was authorized to rate the performance of the teachers, so the assistant superintendent was at least a yearly visitor in each school.

Several teachers, such as Melvin Mack and Mary Strock, remembered going to visit the school directors by turn at their homes when they applied for a job. Mr. Mack recalled going out to the barns to be interviewed by busy farmers who were school directors. Two former teachers recalled their experiences in gaining a position. Mabel Foellner recalled her job application. "When I was about to graduate from normal school, I wrote to our secretary of the school board and asked if there would be any possibility of an opening in our township, because I would be graduating in June, and he wrote back and said there would be one but we can't tell you where it will be.

"You know, you didn't sign contracts months ahead. You took what they gave you and were thankful for it. I didn't know until about a month before the opening of the school term that I would be teaching in Kintnersville."

Iola Parry had completed a teacher preparation program toward the end of the Depression and was interviewed for a position in Williams Township, Northampton County. She was interviewed by the entire board. "Frankly, I didn't think I would get it. It was very casual, and they were very kind and considerate. I was interviewed by the whole board. It wasn't lengthy and they didn't delve deeply. They had your information, statistics, on paper.

"It was held in the school room where you would eventually teach if you were hired. I was sitting in one of the little desks. There was a pencil ledge on the desk and this little bug was crawling there and I was pushing it with a pencil. I wasn't nervous. Frankly, I wasn't too sure I wanted that job when I saw the school way out in the country."

COUNTY EXAM AND EIGHTH-GRADE GRADUATION

As discussed in preceding interviews, in order to enter high school, students from the country schools were required to take and pass a rigorous one-day achievement test, prepared and graded by the county superintendent's office. Anna Neamand was a teacher in Richland Township, and she recalled the county's guidelines.

"At the end of the year we had the county examinations. It stated in our instructions that Bucks County had an examination for all applicants to pass to the ninth grade. The exam was given uniformly throughout the county."

This exam was taken late in the spring of the eighth grade, and evaluated in time to determine the honor students of the graduating class. By about 1910 most of the rural school districts held a graduation ceremony.

The importance of the examination was such that former students recalled the exam vividly, as did Mamie Fluck Kratzer in her interview (Chapter 2). Marian Stumb Renninger told about the county exam as she recalled it in Richland Township.

"At the end of the eighth grade we had to take a test given to us by the county superintendent. That year the children from all of the township schools came to Shelly School to take the test. They could do it all in one school at one time; there weren't that many students. The teachers reported there. The superintendent sent his questions in. He wasn't there himself. The teachers took charge.

"When he had examined the papers, then it was published on the school door who passed and who didn't. I'm telling you that was the day! Some of us didn't have bicycles, but Claude Koder, one in my group, had a bicycle. He said, 'This is the day we're supposed to get the results of the tests. I'm going to keep going up there till it's posted, and I'll tell you. I'll come back.' So he did and came down my street in the township putting his hands up in the air. So we all knew we had passed from our area. But then we had two students who didn't pass from our school. Some thirty-five students took that exam.

"Some of those who didn't pass went to work. You could go to work at that time at fourteen if you had a paper signed by somebody at the school board and a teacher. Or I think if they stayed home and helped their father on the farm they didn't have to have working papers."

Sometimes the students tied in their scores on the exam. Catherine Benner Bleam recalled a novel way in which a tie was broken: "When we graduated from eighth grade, I was the valedictorian. But then the teacher took me aside and said, 'You know, Catherine, you and Eddie Fox were a tie. So to break the tie, your handwriting was better than Eddie's.' They had to break the tie somehow. I told that at the homecoming, and his mother said, 'I still can't read his writing,' and everybody laughed."

GRADUATION CEREMONIES

In Chapter 2 several of the stories included reports of the eighth-grade graduations, including those by Mamie Fluck Kratzer and James Gerhart. Others also had recollections of the graduation ceremony.

James Clemmer, who graduated in 1935 from Richland Township, told us about the graduation ceremony of his eighth-grade township class. "To graduate, there was an exam. All of us eighth-graders went up there to the Shelly School for it. Then after they were graded and we passed we had our graduation exercises up at St. John's Lutheran Church in Quakertown. They had the nicest fellowship hall. We had adult speakers encouraging you on. Then we'd walk up on one side; they'd hand us our diploma, and we'd come down the other."

Mabel Koehler had a copy of the program for her year of graduation, 1931, from Springfield Township. She recalled that, "at the ceremony one child from each school gave a presentation. Examples were poems and essays such as 'Trees,' 'Columbus,' 'The Village Blacksmith,' Lincoln's Gettysburg Address, 'The Sand Piper,' 'How the Game is Played,' 'America's Answer,' and some musical numbers."

TRANSITION TO HIGH SCHOOL

> Derogatory and negative stereotypes (e.g., redneck, hillbilly, hick) frequently blemish descriptions of rural peoples.
> —Alan J. DeYoung and Barbara Kent Lawrence, "On Hoosiers, Yankees, and Mountaineers," *Phi Delta Kappan*, 1995, 108)

When they completed the eighth grade, the students were in early adolescence, and for many the transition from the small country school to the relatively larger and more sophisticated high school was difficult. Many of those whom we interviewed, like Paul Bryan, spoke of anxious and ambivalent feelings when they entered the ninth grade. In several of the stories as seen in Chapter 2 the individuals spoke of the difficulties they felt they faced when they entered ninth grade in a town high school.

Paul Bryan had attended the brand-new Sell-Perk High School in the late 1920s. Mary Dietz attended the neighboring Quakertown High School earlier in the decade. She also felt that the country children were seen as inferior. Like Paul Bryan, her reaction was to prove herself as a student. "Country students were looked down upon by the town students, and I resented it, but that was the attitude. You came from the country, and they thought, 'They can't know very much.' But we just proved to them that we did get what we were supposed to learn.

"Fortunately, I had some very good teachers in the country schools; they were really interested in the children and they tried to help the children get the best education possible. They were all dedicated teachers in the county school. I appreciated that and that's the reason I decided to go back and give them as many possibilities as I could as a teacher, as they had given me. It was a commitment on my part. I went to high school for four years. My marks were all 85 or above."

Glenn Haring attended Quakertown High School in the 1940s. He spoke of the difficulty of adjustment to the comprehensive high school from the small country school. "Going from a one-room school into the ninth grade was a big, big adjustment. Only fourteen kids from the Richland Township schools graduated from high school, and there were thirty-nine that had graduated from the nine one-room schools.

"This is 1940 that I'm talking about. Here you came in from a one-room school with outdoor toilets and outside pump, where you had to carry the coal in. You go into a big consolidated high school where you have big wide corridors and ceramic tile, and these big lavatories. When you get in the homeroom nearly all the kids there know each other because they went to the same school before. And here you are, thrown in with those kids. You don't know anybody. That's a big adjustment.

"We were called 'country hicksters.' You had to make friends with these people and then you were gradually accepted. But if you didn't make friends easily, then you had a problem. I think by about tenth grade we got to know friends and they accepted us. The teachers didn't treat us differently; perhaps they didn't know we were from the country."

Ed Fox had similar impressions about Quakertown High School when he attended in the 1930s. "My most vivid memories about changing schools were going from country school to high school. That was terrible, because when you went to high school from the country school, we felt like foreigners. We were called 'out-of-towners.' It may have just been our imagination, but we felt we were looked down on. We felt we were inferior because we were 'country hicksters.' It took a long time until you got over that feeling."

Marian Stumb Renninger discussed the transition to the high school. She had attended Quakertown High School after graduation from the country school. "It was difficult socially to go to the high school, because the students already had their cliques and they found out that we come from a one-room school house. We weren't in with the group at first; we had to earn our way. We weren't invited to their parties and some of them felt they were more in the in-crowd because they had a little more money than we who were farmers and didn't have a lot of money. You felt this at least through the first year. In the second year I started to make my way. But then I had the misfortune of losing two friends, one who died of TB and another whose mother was always giving her medicine."

Evelyn Hendricks Potter reflected upon the transition to the high school in the 1930s. "There were definite disadvantages. Coming into high school, we had had no athletics at all. With the country schools closing in March, the town kids had school in April and May, so that made a lot of difference. We had no back-ground in science at all. And the fact that we had to change classrooms was a handicap to me too, because I wasn't accustomed to piling up my books and moving from one room to the other. But I don't remember that I thought I couldn't learn. And since my mother was so good at algebra, it was a breeze."

In most of the country schools there was no organized physical education, so ninth-graders from one-room schools generally had no background in team sports, such as basketball, football, or field hockey. The latter was a typical fe-male sport in the high schools of Upper Bucks County.

Lamar Feikel felt that the boys from the country were generally physically stronger than the town boys, which compensated for their lack of early training in team sports. However, he felt that there was discrimination against boys from the country in high school organized athletics at Quakertown High School when he attended in the 1950s. "Not until I got to high school did I see discrimination. That was one of the flaws I saw going to high school. The kids of doctors and lawyers played in the sports. They played the big names and the people with money versus us country hicks. I can vouch for that! They were prechosen; they played the big names. Whether they had financial pull with the school board, who knows. I think there was a lot of politics."

Kay Fox attended Quakertown High School for a year in the 1930s after completing eight grades in the one-room Rock Wild School. "The high school seemed cold, very cold. You didn't know anybody. So many of the children were from town. The country folks had all seemed to be closer. It seemed at the time, although maybe we just thought so, that the town children had so much more than we did. They looked down on us, you know. It was a little crazy when you think of it now. It just didn't have the warmth that the little one-room school did."

Ruth Clemmer Giering graduated from a one-room school in 1937 and from high school in 1941. She recalls high school. "Nobody will realize what it was like for a country kid going to high school. I mean, over in the country school everybody was friendly. When we went to high school starting in ninth grade you felt like an outsider. Believe me you did. It was rough.

"Everybody had their cliques and were always together. They'd say hello to you and things like that, but you could never warm up. I did finally warm up to one girl who lived in Richland Township. But I took the commercial course, and the other girl, who had graduated from our one-room school, took the academic course. The other girl never really got into the other crowd even in the four years. It was really hard, I'll tell you."

Martha Tarantino had a number of obstacles to overcome in going to and staying in high school. She was a farm girl who was needed on the farm. "The biggest adjustment was I had to wear high-top string shoes, and the rest didn't. Mine were laced up to here [her ankles], and the other kids had modern shoes. My grandfather said, 'Girls shouldn't have an education; they're no good after they have an education, you know.' I went two years to high school, but the second year I had to stay home until the corn was husked, so I didn't get the beginning of algebra and Latin. I didn't get the fundamentals. So after the sophomore year I worked at home and started doing housework. I went to work in a shirt factory when I was eighteen."

Arthur Landis had been raised on a dairy farm, and had worked with his father in their dairy. He was disappointed in his course in agriculture in high school and dropped out of high school in the sophomore year.

"I remember the teacher who tried to teach us agriculture. All he knew was what he read out of a book; I could have told him a lot of things he knew without looking in the book. A couple of times he took us out on field trips, one time to a dairy farm. This was a treat for the town kids, but for me it was just the daily routine."

The transition was less dramatic for those students who went to small high schools. Springfield Township had a small high school. Mabel Koehler had gone to a one-room school and then to the township high school. "I don't recall any problems going to high school. It was just a little high school. Four rooms. It wasn't like a city school. There were two rooms upstairs and two downstairs. There were only fourteen that graduated with me. We had four teachers in that high school.

"I found my eighth-grade commencement program. At Springfield in 1931 we had forty-three graduates from the thirteen one-room schools. Out of these forty-three, only fourteen of us graduated from high school. Some didn't even start high school."

Commentary

Various reasons were cited by those who reported difficulty in the transition to high school, the most frequent being the perceived inferior social status of rural people. During most of the period under study, the towns were more modern. The urban areas installed electric systems and public sewers. Electricity came slowly to the farms, and sewerage systems came even later. The majority of farms did not have indoor bathrooms until after World War II and most of the one-room schools never had them. Although there were some wealthy farmers, many farmers, particularly during the Depression, did not live much above a subsistence level. The children had to wear their farm clothing to school, and so they were considered out of style. As Glenn Haring and Ed Fox remarked, they were perceived as "country hicksters."

It was also a transition from the very personal one-room schools to the impersonality of the high schools. As eighth-graders, they had been "top-dogs" in their little schools, often given a great deal of responsibility by the teacher and respect by the smaller students. They went to the bottom of the pecking order in the high schools. The high schools were departmentalized, with specialized teachers teaching the academic subjects, and freshmen who had been used to just one teacher had to respond to the academic expectations of perhaps five or six different teachers. Status in the high school was determined by participation on athletic teams, and many of the country students had never touched a real football, basketball, or baseball, let alone had instruction or practice in team sports.

Early adolescence is a difficult stage of life. It is a time when young people are searching for approval from their age peers. Often the neophyte high school student was the only one from his or her elementary school to come to the high school. They lost the support group of peers from their school. In several cases, our interviewees reported that it took a year before they were accepted.

Whatever the reasons for those who did not complete high school, dropping out in high school or choosing to end formal education after the eighth grade was easier in the first half of the twentieth century than it is now. If they were farm children, there was plenty of work for them to do on the family farm. Except during the Depression when jobs were hard to find, there were plenty of entry-level jobs in grocery stores, factories, and for women, in the many clothing factories of Upper Bucks County. And in many families, the need for the labor of their children on the farms or for the money that adolescents could earn in a factory was more compelling than any future possibilities that could be gained by a high school diploma. As Martha Tarantino mentioned, there was even some feeling among the old Pennsylvania German farmers that too much education ruined the girls. With this attitude, some farm girls did not have much support to continue in high school.

The high school setting was a different culture from that in the small country schools. Insights into that culture were provided by the individuals whom we interviewed, and will be analyzed in the next chapter.

4

Schoolhouse Memories

> Rural schools have traditionally been tightly linked to their com-
> munities. In earlier years, the process of schooling reflected local
> values, local mores, local ways of being in the world. Well into
> this century, rural places had their own ways.
> —Paul Theobald and Paul Nachtigal ("Culture, Community,
> and the Promise of Rural Education," *Phi Delta Kappan*,
> October 1995, 132)

The previous chapter traced the memories of teachers and students about the
academic side of the counry school, where teachers taught lessons from books.
This chapter will probe the memories of the participants about the life that was
lived in the environment of the school. Lessons were "taught" from books. That
was the formal curriculum. Experiences were "caught" from the rich life of the
school; that was a hidden curriculum. There were organic ties with the community that were reflected in the ethos of the school. One of the reasons the one-
room school lasted so long was these organic ties with the rest of rural America.
Memories of the schoolhouse as an environment, of the voluntary support of the
community, and of the kind of culture that flourished and nurtured the school
will be provided in this chapter.

THE SCHOOLHOUSE

> The teacher's desk—an arrangement of frayed books on one end, a
> kerosene lamp on the other—sat on a platform in front of a black-
> board displaying the circles and angled loops of a penmanship
> lesson. To the right of the desk, a small white table held a globe,
> and beyond it sat a potbellied stove, its pipe rising up and across
> the wall, over the alphabet chart. There were windows along the
> two side walls, the daylight bright and hazy through white lace,
> and between the windows, a bookcase or two and a scattering of
> student papers and artwork. As you looked back from the teacher's

> desk to the open door—you entered, as was usually the case,
> through the rear of the classroom—you saw two rows of lunch
> pails, pictures, of Washington and Lincoln.
> —Mike Rose (*Education Week*, March 19, 1997, 38)

Most of the schoolhouses were similar in design. They were one-story, with a porch on the front. The one door into the building was in the middle of the porch. The door opened into a small vestibule, which might have coat hooks for winter wraps. Inside the large single schoolroom there were rows of students' desks. In crowded schools with thirty or more students it was necessary to have double desks where two students would sit together, sharing the same seat and writing surface. The desks were attached to the floor and arranged in rows and, within a row, by size. The smaller children sat toward the front of the room, closest to the teacher's desk, which usually was on a platform, so the teacher could scan the entire classroom from behind his or her desk.

The classroom would be bright on a sunny day, for there were generally three large windows on each side of the room, but they would be dark on cloudy days, for almost none of the country schools had any modern conveniences, until at least the 1930s, when rural electrification began to make electric lighting possible. Most rural school boards did not have the money to install electricity, so in some cases the parents undertook projects to raise the money for the installation. But the schoolchildren were used to pumping water and to outhouses, for most of them did not have modern conveniences at their homes either. Until electrification made automatic water pumps a reality, most farm homes had outside toilets and carried their water from an outside hand pump or from a spring.

Betty Barringer attended a one-room school in Chester County in the 1920s. "The school was lighted by a kerosene light in the middle of the ceiling. The boys sat on one side of the room, girls on the other, younger ones in the front. There was a single entrance to the school through a vestibule, but we hung our coats on hooks in the back of the room. The teacher tended the stove. The boys brought the coal up from the cellar. The bigger girls would go for water at a neighbor's. They cleaned the erasers and blackboard every night. Certain ones were picked to do that. It was a privilege."

Clara Willauer Kipp recalled the room arrangements in Shaw's School in Richland Township, Bucks County, during the 1920s. "The boys sat on one side of the room and the girls on the other. The stove was in the middle. Between the boys and the girls there was an empty aisle. We got drinking water from a pump beside the school building. I think they brought buckets of water into the schoolroom. And there was a ladle. As a rule the teacher tended the stove. Sometimes the teacher would have a boy from the area come early and open the school and heat it. We had a coal bin and a wood bin attached to the rear of the school building. The room was comfortable, but the clothes closets were very cold. They were right as you entered the school. The boys had their wraps on the left side; the girls on the right."

Melvin Mack, a teacher at Tylersport, Montgomery County, in 1935–37, described his school: "We had no water; we had outside toilets; and we had no electricity. We had about six kerosene lamps hanging around the wall, which we used only in cloudy weather. Really they didn't do much good, just three on one side, three on the other."

Many of the schools were close to farms. The farms operated year-round. Dairy farmers used the manure from their stables to fertilize their crops. Iola Parry described the farm odors that infiltrated her country school in Williams Township, Northampton County. "Our school was isolated. The lane leading to the school was dirt. You could not see a house from there. In fact, this is humorous. In the spring you had to close the windows because they were fertilizing the fields, and you just couldn't stand it. Sometimes the boys would come in with it on their shoes. The aroma was very strong."

Schools would be closed up during the summer from May until the end of August. In many cases, weeds would be allowed to grow on the school yard and there was no activity in the school until it was time for school to start right after Labor Day. In some cases the school directors would get the schools in shape for the school term. At other times, local citizens would be hired to get the school building in order. Mabel Foellner recalled the preparation of her school at Kintnersville for the fall term. "I was told that two people from the village would clean the school before the fall term. The walls were whitewashed; the windows were washed; the weeds were cut, and all of the repairs were made. All of the seats were fastened to the floors, and your floors were oiled."

Rochelle Renninger Boyle recalled the three schools she attended in the 1950s, all of which were similar. "I remember in our entranceways we always had a big front porch. It was cement. Then there was the coatroom where we hung our hats and coats. There were all those jagged coat hooks. There always got to be so much pushing and shoving in there all the time. The teacher was always saying, 'Be careful you don't jab your eyes out,' or something like that. It was always so cold in there because there was no heat.

"We had single desks. On some the lid lifted up; with the others you cramped down and you just shoved your stuff into them. We didn't have inkwells. They were gone, because ballpoint pens came in. Holes were left in the desk where the inkwells had gone. My husband remembers pulling the pigtails of the girl in front of him, then tying them in the hole, because there was no ink in them. The boys would stick a pencil through the pigtail so the girls couldn't pull away, and they had their head held back there."

VOLUNTARISM

In many cases, parents or local citizens made unusual contributions of labor or money toward the activities of one-room schools. One of the most remarkable was described in an earlier section, when Carrie Horne told how a Parent-Teacher Association provided a playground for the students of the Passer School. In many cases there was a formal organization that held evening meetings of the parents. These were called PTAs, although they were generally not affiliated with the national PTA.

But they did other things, as well. As Carrie Horne explained, "We had a very active PTA. They were really, really marvelous. They got together and they put a water system into our school. We had a very good well with a pump, but it was outside. They decided that there was space enough underneath the pump to dig out to put in an electric pump, and then to have two basins, one in each of the classrooms. With volunteer help they did the wiring. We bought basins and fountains to use inside in each one of the rooms, so we had running water, finally.

"How did we make the money? Well, the money was made by a carnival which we gave over at the old high school. And for entertainment they had a team on the radio that was very, very popular. We drew terrific crowds and made a lot of money on that.

"Before that we had decided that our playground was much too small. Through the efforts of our PTA president, Mark Mease, who was also our bus driver, we decided to go to see Mr. Soltisiak, who owned the field next to the school and see if we couldn't buy some land. It was good farmland and good road frontage, but we were lucky enough to have his son in my room at that time and Steve just loved baseball. So we went to ask Mr. Soltisiak whether we could buy three acres. And he said, 'The kids must have a place to play, so I'll sell you three acres.' 'Well, how much do you want?' Well, he guessed seven hundred dollars. Well, I shook in my shoes because I knew how much the PTA had in its treasury. But Mark said, 'We'll take it.' We took it and we managed to pay it off. We sold different things and paid that off.

"Instead of deeding it to the school board, because it was definitely bought with PTA funds, not taxpayer funds, the deed was written not to the school board, but to the PTA. I found out later that it was the other teacher and I who owned the property. We don't own it anymore, but it made it very convenient when it came to buying the schoolhouse and making it into a community center as we later did when the new high school was built. So we did have an active PTA."

Anna Neamand taught in a school that did not have electricity. She tells how the PTA raised the money for electrification of the school building. "Toward the end of the Depression, in 1935 or 1936, we had a wonderful rapport with the parents. We began having evening programs, one a month, really, and there was no electricity. The first one was Christmas. No electricity in the building. We had an organ you could either pump with your feet, or you could have one of the boys pump the handles.

"Talking it over with some of the parents, we decided that we would take a collection the night of the Christmas program. The money would be used to buy a piano and install electricity. The parents came and installed temporary electricity with long extension cords, all the way to the neighbor's barn, so we had lights for the Christmas program. The crowd was so large they stood outside on the porch shoulder to shoulder and at all the windows. Inside there was no room to get another one in to stand. We had a collection that evening of almost $225. In the Depression! So you see the parents supported the school and were proud of their children."

There was a fringe benefit of the evening programs, as Anna Neamand explained. "We found out who the good cooks were. Oh, my, we had good food after the meetings. The parents would bring cakes, and they were proud. Fourteen cakes, sometimes, for one evening!"

The parents helped in the life of the school in other ways, she remembered. "The floorboards were worn; the wind would scatter through. It was quite cold on

Christmas program, Wimmer's School, 1936. Evening programs were presented for meetings of the Parent-Teacher Association (PTA). The children were in costume for the Christmas program as described by Miss Neamand. Photo reproduced courtesy of Miss Anna Neamand.

the floor in the winter time. So the parents installed a floor diagonally across the old floor.

"At Christmas, a big red cedar tree, which reached the ceiling, was brought in. Parents and children went along one Saturday morning to one parent's woodland and cut the tree. So we put the tree up on a Saturday morning. Oh, the aroma of that tree for the next week was delicious! I can still enjoy it so many years later. I think there's nothing like the aroma of a red cedar tree when it gets hot."

Glenn Haring attended another school in Richland Township that did not have electricity. The parents decided to help. "When I went to the country school, we didn't have lights, none at all. The school board would not put them in; they had no money. The only way lights were put into our one-room school was through the efforts of the PTA. I know, my father was on the PTA, and he decided that maybe if they could do an Amos and Andy Show they could get enough money. My dad took the part of the Kingfish. They blacked up their faces. They raised enough money to put in lights. That might have been about 1933, right in the middle of the Depression.

"Each school had its own PTA. PTAs were very active then. They were cooperative in those days, unlike some now causing trouble."

Marion Stumb Renninger described how her mother helped the teacher in her school to obtain a better piano. "We had a real old melodeon piano at school, and it was so bad the music didn't come forth like it should. When Mrs. Jacoby King came to school as the teacher she thought it would be so nice if we could have another piano. My mother went door to door where they had pupils in the school collecting nickels or quarters, whatever they could give, until she got the fifty dollars for a used upright piano. She got it together in a short time, and I played the piano for the class."

Commentary

The one-room schools could not have been operated so inexpensively if it had not been for another group of volunteers who are seldom recognized, the members of the school board. The small rural school districts had school boards composed of six members, elected for terms of six years. Only one of the members received a salary, the school board secretary, selected from among the elected members. He or she received a small yearly stipend. The secretary was the executive officer of the board. Not only did the secretary keep minutes of the meetings, he or she was responsible for obtaining the teachers' supplies, seeing that the teachers had contracts, and handling all correspondence (Leight, 1990).

Given the attitudes of the times, most school directors were men, although women were eligible to serve after the Nineteenth Amendment to the Constitution (1920) gave them the right to vote. However, in Richland Township it was not until 1937 that the first woman, Louella Whalen, was elected to the board of school directors. She was elected to serve as vice president at the meeting in which she was sworn in on December 6, 1937, according to the minutes of the school board of Richland Township.

Money was scarce in the rural areas, particularly during the Great Depression of the 1930s. School boards had difficulty raising enough money to pay the teachers, let alone to make capital improvements. Through the voluntary efforts of individuals and groups such as the PTAs, some fortunate schools were gradually able to enjoy improvements.

CHORES

There were no janitors in the little country schools. All of the routine tasks such as cleaning the classroom and providing heat and water had to be done either by the teacher or the students. Several of those we interviewed had memories of helping with the classroom chores.

Emma Weirbach attended a school near Ottsville prior to World War I. She described the cooperation of teacher and students in performing school tasks. She also described one change in the school environment caused by the migration of well-to-do, urban families into the region. "We washed the blackboard on a Friday. Some students were sent out to clap the erasers. We all helped to sweep up the floors. The teacher would be sweeping, too. We all worked together.

"We had an outside toilet. We didn't have to clean those. Later on we didn't have to go outside any more. The New York and Philadelphia people were starting to move in and then we had a toilet in the school in the corner with chemicals. We cleaned that once a week. Those city children were what started this. To go outside to a bathroom was awful for them."

Kay Fox recalled several jobs that the students did to keep the school functioning smoothly. "We had a big heater in the corner of the schoolroom which had a big water jacket around it. The boys would have to bring in the wood to start the fire, while the others were outside cleaning the erasers if they didn't get them all done the night before. That was the chores in the morning [*sic*]. After school different ones, usually the boys, would have to sweep. Sweep out all the dirt and the pussies [dust balls] under the desks, and all that sort of thing. We all had our little jobs.

"The building was a stone building, with a bell on top. Oh, that was another advantage. Oh, my. If you knew your lessons and were a good kid in the school in those days we got a lot of little jobs we were proud to do. We could stand at the back, at the door, and ring the bell for the children to come in. Then you put your finger up to your mouth and you said, 'Sh.' Everybody had to come in quietly. This, of course, made us feel really good. We were allowed to do this and help the teacher, and she was glad that we could do it while she was doing something else."

Rochelle Renninger Boyle recalled the assignment of chores. "Usually one of the bigger boys tended the fires. One of their jobs was to bring the coal in from the outside bin in the morning. The girls at the end of each day brushed all the dirt along our row to the end of the row, in the aisles and around our desks. I don't remember if that was every day or once a week. Because the floors were all oiled it was a dirty job. There were no janitors."

With no running water, drinking water was either obtained from a pump on the school ground or by going to a neighbor who had a water pump or a spring.

Emma Weirbach spoke of the division of labor in her school. "The boys would bring the coal in. We had to bring our buckets of water. We would get our water to a farm [*sic*] below the school. We took a bucket and stick and with one on each end we would go down there and bring a bucket of water and put it in the cooler. The girls did that mostly. The boys brought the coal in."

Kay Fox too told about a different gender-based assignment and also about a communal sharing. "We had a bucket of water in the back of the room on the window sill with one dipper in it. That was drinking water from the well. One of the biggest boys would have to go out and bring the water in. Everybody drank out of the dipper. Aside [*sic*] of that was a wash basin and a little bar of soap on a jar lid. That's where you washed your hands, and one towel the teacher would bring. Everybody would use it, a clean towel. Everybody would drink out of the same dipper. And we were all healthy."

Commentary

Many people used the analogy of a "family" in describing the culture of the one-room school. In the busy but routine tasks of maintaining the schoolroom the relationships were like those of a family. The teacher, like a parent, had the authority to assign tasks and to monitor their completion. The teacher-pupil relationships became more informal as students performed jobs similar to those that they did at home with their parents and other siblings.

Although there are a few exceptions in the examples given above, the jobs tended to be assigned by gender roles. Boys did the heavy work of carrying coal or wood and tending the fire; girls did most of the cleaning.

Perhaps the most important lesson learned was that everyone needed to help to maintain the physical environment of the school. Technically, the teacher was responsible for the cleanliness and orderliness of the schoolroom. Willing hands made the work lighter and permitted the teacher to pay more attention to instruction. Having an opportunity to go outside to clap erasers was a relief from the enclosed space of the classroom for the students. There were informal transactions going on as chores were assigned and completed. The teacher could be less strict. Students could vie for the best "jobs."

THE STOVE

A space heater was a major feature in each schoolhouse. Wood and hard coal were the types of locally available fuels for the furnaces, as all of southeastern Pennsylvania was within range of the anthracite coal mines of the northeastern coal region.

It was the responsibility of the teacher to maintain the fire. Some of the heaters were potbellied stoves placed in the middle of the schoolroom. By the 1920s a more modern type of furnace with a "jacket," or sheet metal cover, began to be installed, replacing the old potbellied stoves. They could be placed in a back corner of the schoolroom, which improved traffic flow and teacher visibility in the center of the classroom.

Even the more modern stoves were crude compared to heaters today. They had no thermostats, so the draft was adjusted manually. They had to be started with wood; when the wood fire was hot enough the coal could be ignited. If they were banked properly a fire would burn overnight, but would be allowed to go out on a Friday afternoon. In order to have the room warm on a chilly Monday someone would have to start a new fire and have it burning well on Sunday afternoon.

Anna Neamand recalled dealing with the stove in Wimmer's School. "When I got my job, the credentials were all right, but I was cautioned, you must know how to make fire and keep the floor clean. So I was determined that we were not going to be cold. The second week of school I built a coal fire, and it was hot. I didn't know how to regulate it too well, so one night after school I went to Quakertown and bought eight window screens. That served two purposes—got a little air inside and kept the flies out.

"We continued organizing and having a good time together. By the end of my term at Wimmer's, six years, all the boys from grades six, seven, and eight knew how to make coal fire. I didn't have to even look at the stove. They liked it."

Rochelle Renninger Boyle described how the stove was used for other purposes than heating the room. "We had coal stove in Rocky Ridge School and Scholl's School. I know if the fire had gone out in the night it would take longer to warm up in the morning. Always bring in potatoes and put them in an hour or so before lunchtime, put them on top of the stove and then the kids would have baked potatoes for lunch.

"There was a little crick [sic] behind Scholl's School and every once in a while someone would fall in. Then the person would have to sit behind the coal stove and dry out there and he could still be in his lessons."

James Clemmer told us about culinary uses of the stove by Mrs. Florence Fluck. "The stove was off to the side of the room. When Mrs. Fluck was there she would buy things like you'd use for a cookout. We would put our egg sandwiches and things and hold them above the flames; roast them over the coal fire, in a little handheld grill of wire.

"We used to carry in the coal, and take out the ashes. There was no janitor. They had a new type of stove and they would hold the fire over, I believe, though maybe Mrs. Fluck went down on Sundays and kept the fire going. I don't recall that. It was always warm when we got there."

Kay Lowman explained about preparing lunch at the Springfield School. "At lunchtime we would bring in a can of soup and put it on the coal heater to heat up the soup. We could bring potatoes to bake, sometimes, and put them in the heater, also. We'd heat the soup right in the can."

Harold Koder recalled when the potbellied stove was replaced by a more modern furnace in the early 1920s. "There was a different kind of heater, which was called a pipeless heater. That was a larger stove that they put in the corner of the building, rather than in the center. There you could open its door and put a can of soup inside. You didn't dare close the door completely. The soup would get hot."

Arthur Landis remembered another use of the stove. "We had the furnace in the middle of the schoolroom, and of course if any children would come with wet socks they'd take them off and hang them on the metal shield until they were dry."

Florence Vogt attended schools in Hilltown Township. "I was a great eater and sometimes another girl and I would spend our school lunch hour eating. We carried our lunches. No such thing as a cafeteria. In the front of the stove was a big grate, very, very large. Inside of this we could put potatoes and they would bake. We could put soup in containers and it would get hot."

Ralph Koehler attended the Central School in Richland Township. Both his mother and his father were teachers there at different times. He recalled an innovation at the time his mother was a teacher. "There were of course no cafeterias in the country schools, but I think it was when my mother was a teacher there—I don't know if it was her idea alone or whether parents got together—but on certain days some kids would bring milk and other things to make soup. So you had hot soup every so often, maybe once or twice a week. I think we had a kerosene stove. Some of the farmers in the area would donate the milk, I think."

The opportunity to have hot food for lunch was a luxury in the rural schools. Students and teachers experimented with ingenious ways to use the potbellied stoves or space heaters to bake potatoes, heat canned food, or grill sandwiches over an open fire. A few teachers, such as Mrs. Koehler and Mrs. Strunk, brought in a small kerosene range to cook soup or hot cocoa.

Ed Fox felt that Mrs. Laura Strunk was a pioneer in the provision of hot lunches. "I think that Mrs. Strunk was one of the pioneers, one of the first teachers in the area to institute hot lunch. We had a kerosene stove in the back of the room. The Landises had a dairy farm and they brought milk, and then we'd have hot chocolate. Usually the older girls would start the stove before lunchtime. They were delegated to go to the back of the room and start preparing the hot cocoa. And that was the origin of the hot school lunch. "It went good, too. It tasted good."

The smell of food left an impression. More than forty-five years after she had taught in a one-room school, Iola Parry recalled the aroma. "One of the

things that still remains poignant in my mind is that the children used to bring
their lunches for all-day school. They used to like to toast their sandwiches in
the potbellied stove. They had this long rod with a frame on the end of it. Their
sandwiches used to be bologna for the most part, and onion, so around noontime
it got pretty raunchy in there.

"The stove was located to the right of the teacher's desk. I know that in
the bitter cold weather I would be inclined to move over toward the stove. The
far end of the room was cold. You couldn't rotate the children because you had to
have the wee ones in the front because they had to work together."

The smells from the furnace were not always those of food being
toasted. William Steers told of a way of getting out of school. "We had a great
big stove for heat. I couldn't get my arms around it. It had a shield. On really
cold days you'd get up close to it. It didn't throw much heat. It was a coal stove.
The coal bin was just outside. The bigger boys filled a big bucket with coal and
carried it in. When we wanted to get out of school one of the boys would urinate
on the coal. So the teacher had to let us go, because of the stink."

Commentary

By contrast, contemporary homes and schoolrooms have central heating and
often air conditioning. Temperature and humidity are controlled by thermostats.
Except for paying the bills and ensuring that routine maintenance is done, the
modern home pays little attention to its heating needs. Modern schools have
custodians who see that the schoolrooms are warm and comfortable with central
heating for the entire multi-room building.

But in the schools of yesterday, life was not that easy for the teacher and the
students. The teacher had to learn to operate the old potbellied stove or space
heater. Students were entrusted with some of the tasks of building and maintaining the fires. These tasks were often seen as privileges earned by the older students. Further, as told above, ingenious teachers and students found ways of using the stove to vary their school lunches by baking potatoes and by roasting
sandwiches or by heating soup. In a real sense, the old stove was not just a part
of the school environment, it was a part of the learning experience of the old
country school.

TRAVEL TO SCHOOL

The school-house which stood at the corner of our new farm was
less than half a mile away, and yet on many of the winter days
which followed, we found it quite far enough . . . but nothing except a blizzard . . . could keep us away from school. Facing the cut-
ting wind, wallowing through the drifts, battling like small in-
trepid animals, we often arrived at the door moaning with pain yet
unsubdued, our ears frosted, our toes numb in our boots, to meet
others in similar case around the roaring hot stove.
—Hamlin Garland (*A Son of the Middle Border*, 1914, 111)

The climate in southeastern Pennsylvania was not so severe as Garland recalled about winter on the Middle Border, but children had to get to school in the

same way in the early twentieth century. Many spoke of walking to school in snowy weather.

Many schoolchildren today arrive at school by the omnipresent yellow school bus, whereas students had to get to the country school by a number of modes of travel, for school buses were not available to most of them before school consolidation. The most prevalent way was to walk, although if the children lived a great distance from the school or if the weather was bad, other alternatives were found.

James Clemmer told of coming to school in the 1920s. "Some mornings my mother would drive us to school. We had a car, and four kids who lived further away would arrive at our house just about in time, so we had a car full. But we always walked home in the evening, unless the weather was real bad. If there was a lot of snow, we enjoyed walking home in the deep snow. I remember a couple of times when the roads were real icy we skated to school right on the roads. To get to school we wore Arctics [boots] of cloth and they buckled in the front."

Emma Weirbach was a farm girl who did not have access to an automobile. "If the snow was too deep we wouldn't go. If there were just a few inches we'd walk. When it was snowing my mother would put a veil over my face when it was real bad, and you put stockin's [sic] up over your shoes when it snowed. In the beginning I used to wear homemade shoes. My brother had Arctics. Cotton stockin's, cotton dresses. Little girls wore stockin's most all the time. In wintertime, gosh, you had to wear long underwear.

"When you got to school it wasn't warm in there. Your hands were so cold in the winter when we'd get there we'd have to warm our hands up by the stove. Your hands would be so cold you couldn't work. So sometimes we didn't get started until late."

Mary Weikel's parents had to walk to work early, so they took her to a neighbor's home, where she and her siblings stayed until it was time to go to school. "My parents walked to work. We stayed at a farmer's house until schooltime. The mother and the grandmother that lived at the place took care of us. We all got up early, because my parents had to start work at six. I remember my dad would put me in an express wagon. He used to pull us on that to the farmhouse over dirt roads. When it rained, we had an oilcloth over us. We stayed at the farmhouse until it was time to go to school."

Kay Lowman had these memories about going to school in snowy weather: "We'd walk from our farm, which was about a mile from the school. I remember that our neighbor, Charles Melchoir, came out one day in the snowdrifts and picked me up with my sister and took us to school on horseback when it was snowing. I remember that quite vividly. There must have been three of us on the horse, two children plus the grown-up."

Often the distance to school was greater when students went to high school. Grace Knapp tells of going from their dairy farm to Hilltown High School in Blooming Glenn. "My brother and I went together. He and I used to take the milk on the way to school. We had a wagon and horse and buggy and took milk to the creamery and then we went to school. Then we put the horse in a barn which was near the school during the day. The horse was unhitched from the wagon and put in a stall. When it was time to go home, then we hitched the horse up again and went on home. There were others who did the same thing. One fellow I know, he used to ride a horse to school."

Marian Stumb Renninger got a ride on a milk wagon when the weather was bad. "Our neighbor, Mr. Koder, had a milk business, and he was finished with his route by the time that school started. In bad weather, he would let us all pile into his milk wagon and he would take us to school. Of course we had to stand. Some ten of us including several of his own children would be on the wagon. Mrs. Koder would bundle us all up. After school in bad weather he would come and get us, too, many times. He was the only one who had horses at the time in our neighborhood. That was in the 1910s. We didn't have a family car then."

Marian Stumb Renninger also told about the type of warm clothing that girls wore in the pre–World War I period. "In order to keep warm we wore under-drawers, long legged underwear. They had a panty-top to them. Then full-length stockings and we wore a garter belt that held the stockings up. Oh, it was a terrible thing to get dressed in the morning. It was awful. The stockings were of black cotton. I never liked them.

"I remember I fell into the Tohickon Creek once and the Koder boy pulled me out. It was deep water and sort of icy at that time. We were on our way to school. I went home and Mother got me stripped right away and clean clothes on [sic]."

Clara Willauer Kipp recalled walking to school during the timeframe of World War I. "I don't remember school ever being called off for the weather, but I do remember walking through very, very deep snow. We wore black fabric leggin's, button down the sides of the legs and strap underneath the foot."

William Steers also remarked on cold weather styles in the pre–World War I period. "Sometimes the snow was eighteen inches deep. We had hip boots. The girls had boots too. In the wintertime they used to wear this long underwear, and they hated that, because they couldn't get it on right. Things would be fluffed up in the back. And black cotton stockings. The girls wore bloomers too."

Jim Clemmer told about an adventure on his way home from school. "The Tohickon Creek used to flood and the creek froze over. One winter a friend of mine and I wanted to test the ice. We walked out quite far and we broke in. This was on the way home from school. I remember we were paddling like mad, and we got out. I remember getting a pretty good reprimand when I got home. I was a little scared as well as cold because it was quite deep. The creek was at least twenty-feet wide."

Catherine Benner Bleam told about going to school in bad weather. "We walked to school, except in bad weather my dad would take us in an old Model-T Ford. Around seventh grade in the winter we had an awful blizzard. The roads were closed and my father said, 'You can't go to school. You have no golashes.'

"Well, I loved school. I said, 'I want to go to school.' He says, 'All right. If you put on my old tacky leggin's you can go to school.' He thought I'd be too proud. I went and put them on so he had to let me walk to school. They were like old army leggin's, all laced up. There were only eight kids in school that day."

Commentary

Unless there was bad weather, most families could not even consider any alternative to walking. Although roads were often unpaved, traffic was light and the countryside was considered safe.

The country schools almost never closed for bad weather, unless creeks were flooded or snow was so deep it made roads impassable for foot or horse travel. Adventurous students found inviting side excursions, such as those described by James Clemmer.

Later on, school consolidation required bus transportation and an elaborate system of safeguards for the children. Bad road conditions mean that school is called off or delayed. The acceptance by educational policymakers of an obligation to transport children to and from school has resulted in incredible financial costs that would have astounded school board members and taxpayers in the pre-consolidation age.

VALUES AND ATTITUDES

Many teachers and students referred to the values they felt were learned in the one-room school, both "taught" and "caught," that were the standards in the culture of their childhood. The microcosm of the schoolhouse was a reflection of the macrocosm of rural society.

They recalled that the parents supported the teachers. Iola Parry recalled the attitudes of farm families in the 1930s. "One year I had four children from one family. One was an eighth-grader and one a first-grader. One day this little one had his arms up in the air, making noises, and his big brother way in the back yelling, 'Stevie, stop it. Stevie.' So you know the children helped discipline each others. So I would say the rapport was excellent. They kind of looked after the younger ones; though not so much unless they were brothers and sisters.

"I'm talking about the attitudes of the 1930s. If you don't behave in school you're going to have it from your parents. So that helped the rapport and discipline in every way. Today, I think there is now a more defensive attitude. Some parents today will say, 'Well, what's wrong with the teacher?' I hear from teachers today that the parent is apt to say, 'Well, I can't do anything with him either.'"

Florence Vogt had this comment about the parents' attitudes toward teachers. "Sometimes I think the kids would be better off going back to one-room schools. Today, life is such a fast pace. They are making it too complicated today.

"It was an advantage to have the same teacher for several years. It didn't make any difference if the teacher liked you or not. Your parents made sure that you were there. Today, parents say, 'Oh, my kid doesn't get along with that teacher so I'm going to pull him out.' But that didn't make any difference. Your parents said, 'You do it; and you did it.'

"Our parents taught us to be respectful of the teacher and other people. That's one thing I can say. We wouldn't think of talking back like the kids do today. No way, to your parents or the teachers. Both. That was just a natural thing. It came from your parents. It also came from your Sunday school teachers. It came from everyone. Today it doesn't."

Until the mid-1960s, all public schools in Pennsylvania opened the school day with the reading of ten verses from the Bible and the recitation of the Lord's Prayer. Most of those interviewed felt that some reference to religion was a good thing. Robert Tarantino recalled the influence of this practice.

"I know there are some pupils today that don't get a chance to go to church. But when they went to school they had at least the Bible reading. The families that never went to church or Sunday school didn't get anything of the word of God except at school. This meant something to me in my younger days. The teacher read it, and then we as a group gave the Lord's Prayer. And that's the way it should be today; those that don't want to participate, they don't have to say it."

Rochelle Renninger Boyle felt that religion was taught in school and she reflected upon her beliefs. "We had Bible reading and prayer all through my twelve grades. In grade school the teacher read the Bible. In junior high the kids all took turns. I remember hearing about evolution and the prehistoric stuff, but not until seventh grade. That was a whole new concept to me then. I was fascinated by it. But then I thought, 'Well, I don't care how God did it. God did it.' That's the way I resolved it. He could do it."

Lamar Feikel commented on the treatment of religion in one-room schools. "Religion was brought in many times. When we went to high school they kind of drifted away from the religious part of the education. But out in the country if they threw in fifteen minutes of Bible reading the kids listened. Most of us went to church Sunday anyway. Our parents required it."

Catherine Benner Bleam recalled a lesson in patriotism and some hard lessons about her parents' attitudes toward too much formal education. "William Jennings Bryan was one of Mrs. Strunk's idols, and so in our history lesson she asked us who he was. Well, I guess sometimes I was naughty. I said, 'Well, he ran for president, didn't make it, and had to run back again.' Oh, did she get mad! I just wanted to make everybody laugh.

"She was very patriotic. I remember it was Calvin Coolidge's inauguration, when we were going to school. A lot of us didn't have a radio. So she left [*sic*] us go to one of the pupil's home and listen to the inauguration, just the upper grades, during schooltime. She stayed with the school. She left us go by ourselves. We were glad to go. My parents were old Mennonites and they didn't believe in radios."

Although Catherine Benner Bleam was the valedictorian of her school district she was not allowed to go to the graduation ceremony. "There were six from my school to graduate from eighth grade. I think they all went on to high school except me. Graduation was held in the Grange Hall. To tell you the truth, I wasn't allowed to go. My folks said it was against their religion. I had never joined their church. They belonged to Church of God Mennonites. It broke my heart. Mrs. Strunk was really upset. As valedictorian I was to make a little speech. It was called, 'Life Is a Picture, So Paint It Well.' I never asked if somebody else read it at graduation.

"I wanted to go to high school, but Dad didn't let the boys go either. He said you get too proud and don't have enough humility when you get education. 'You need humility,' he said. But I had really enjoyed going to school."

Commentary

The attitude of the Amish toward education is well known. They believe that an education beyond the eighth grade will make a person "worldly." Apparently the parents of Catherine Benner Bleam were of a closely related Mennonite group, so she was not permitted to participate in the graduation ceremony nor to continue her education beyond the eighth grade.

A source of informal education and a social center for farm families was the Patrons of Husbandry, popularly called the "Grange." Local granges had weekly meetings. They provided an opportunity for farm families to meet other rural folks and to be entertained by a literary program. They had other social events, such as strawberry festivals. The State Grange was an advocate of rural people to state government. Of interest to rural people were issues such as the construction of all-weather roads, rural electrification, rural postal delivery, and similar issues.

Richland Grange Number 1206 was located next to the Shelly School. It was on a main highway in a central location in the township; it had an ample meeting room. Until about 1930 most Richland Township eighth-grade graduations were held in the Grange Hall. After that date they were held in churches in two boroughs in the township, Quakertown or Richlandtown. The churches had more spacious meeting rooms.

THE GAMES THEY PLAYED: FUN AT RECESS

> Fifteen minutes were all too short for them to play. . . . I let recess
> extend five minutes so they could finish their second games. . . .
> And my . . . pupils played this game with all the enthusiasm and
> spirit they had! They put themselves into it—every pupil in
> school. Not one stood by to watch. Because they were having the
> time of their lives, I hated to ring the bell for "books."
> —Jesse Stuart (*The Thread that Runs So True*, 1949, 6)

One of the perennial jokes about elementary schools is that the favorite subject is recess. If the "three Rs" inside the classroom were reading, 'riting, and 'rithmetic, the "fourth R" outside the classroom was "recess." Certainly the children and young adolescents in the country schools were like students everywhere in looking forward to the chance to escape the confines of their desks and formal lessons for an opportunity for unstructured play. Typically, they had a fifteen-minute recess both in the morning and afternoon and an hour lunch period. Most hurried through their lunches in good weather to get outside to play.

Most school yards had no commercial playground equipment, so students were inventive in creating their own amusements for the lunch hour and the two recesses. Although the schools were isolated, schoolchildren often played essentially the same games in different schools under different names.

An almost universal game required the children to form teams on either side of the schoolhouse and throw a rubber ball over the pitched roof. This game was called by such names as "Giggely Over," "Anthony Over" (or "Antony Over"), "Wally Over," and "Tickely Over."

This game must have been played in many parts of the country, and over a long period of time in the little schools. Edward Eggleston, in his *The Hoosier School-Boy*, described a game played in Indiana late in the nineteenth century:

I suppose there are boys in these days who do not know what "Anthony-over" is. How, indeed, can anybody play Anthony-over in a crowded city?

The old one-story village school-houses stood generally in an open green. The boys divided into two parties, the one going on one side, and the other on the opposite side of the school-house. The party that had the ball would shout "Anthony!" The others responded, "Over!" To this, answer was made from the first party, "Over she comes!" and the ball was immediately thrown over the school-house. If any of the second party caught it, they rushed, pell-mell, around both ends of the school-house to the other side, and that one of them who held the ball essayed to hit some one of the opposite party before they could exchange sides. If a boy was hit by the ball thus thrown he was counted as captured to the opposite party, and he gave all his efforts to beat his old allies. So the game went on, until all the players of one side were captured by the others. I don't know what Anthony means in this game, but no doubt the game is hundreds of years old, and was played in English villages before the first colony came to Jamestown. (Eggleston, 1898, 48–49)

This game, or a variation of it, was played in many sections of the country in the old one-room schools. The rules might have been modified to fit the particular school, just as the name varied from school to school in southeastern Pennsylvania. By the twentieth century, girls played along with the boys.

Emma Weirbach began school near Ottsville in about 1911. "When there was snow we would go sledding in a field near the school and our teacher would give us ten or fifteen minutes longer at noontime. Sometimes Mr. Frankenfield would come out and help, but most of the time we played by ourselves. We used to play 'Antony Over.' The one who caught the small rubber ball would try to catch you, tag you with the ball or throw it to tag you. The boys and the girls played these games together. We all mixed together."

We asked Mary Hager Dietz about playground activities when she was in a country school in the 1920s. "The older ones were thoughtful. They used to take care of you. The big ones were very understanding. All ages used to play practically the same kind of games. I remember playing 'Tickeley Over.' That was a lot of fun and mixed ages could play that.

"The little ones would play with their own baseballs. I remember making many of those rag balls. It was a soft ball, and we'd take a board for a bat. The only equipment was what you brought yourself. Nothing else, no swings or anything."

Mabel Foellner had been a student in a rural school during World War I and returned as a teacher in the same area during the 1920s and 1930s. She spoke of how the bigger students helped the little ones and how, when teaching in a one-room school, she found it necessary to supervise the playground activities to be sure that all the children were involved. "Because they were such different ages that had to learn to play games together, I would go out and see that the smaller group had something to do, and the bigger ones had something. You were helping each other as much as you could.

"In the wintertime, when there'd be snow on the ground, they'd make as big a circle as they could, trotting around, and then they'd cross in the middle. 'Ring-tag,' they called it. Another game was 'Anthony Over.' At Revere, it was a two-story building, so it was quite an achievement to get the ball over it. A window got broken once in a while, but not too often.

"Another game was 'Kick the Rickie.' In it, a stick was propped up against the flagpole. You would kick the stick, and while the person who was 'It' was getting the stick, you would hide. Then he'd have to hunt you. If you could go 'home' and touch the base before he did, then you were free.

"The older boys shot marbles in the spring of the year. There was no pave-ment, so they played in the dirt. They'd make a circle in the dirt. Not many girls played marbles, just a few tomboys. That was considered to be a boy's game."

In another rural community about twenty miles to the west, Marvin Rosen-berger was enrolled in a school in Milford Township. He remembered playing games during lunch hour and recess similar to those played in the schools where Mabel Foellner was the teacher. A game similar to that which the children at Revere called "Anthony Over" was played in his school as "Giggely Over." "Kick the Rickie" was similar to "Kick the Wicket" in Marvin Rosenberger's school. Like students in all of the schools the students in Milford township took advantage of the sports of the various seasons. Marvin Rosenberger recalled: "At recess we went out and played some games. We played 'Giggely Over.' Another game we called 'Kick the Wicket.' We'd have a piece of bicycle tire propped up against the chimney and we'd try to kick it away. Then we'd have baseball games in the spring. I remember a time when we were taken over to Rosedale for a baseball game with pupils at Rosedale School.

"I remember one winter at the edge of the school there was a meadow. Up through the meadow, it was flooded and it made a big sheet of ice, and we all brought our ice skates. A lot of the time we went ice skating at lunch. Even at recess we went out there. I still have that pair of skates that I bought from the hardware store in Spinnerstown, a pair of old clamp-on skates."

Kay Fox had been a student at a school in a wooded and rocky region of Upper Bucks County. We asked her what she did over the lunch period. "Well, there were a lot of kiddies right around school, including myself, who could go home for lunch. But we liked the idea of sitting on a great big rock or under a tree. We had a line fence along the edge of the school yard, and there were great big rocks, and we'd sit on these rocks and have our lunch. We'd bring napkins and a little bag or a lunchbox, and we'd share our lunch with each other. All the things you couldn't do if you went to another school. We preferred to do that and enjoyed it very much.

"Then after lunch we'd play games. My friend and I would high jump and we'd get a couple of kids to hold the rope up. We got to five feet and jumped over it. We thought that was great. Some kids would play ball. We played 'Giggely Over.' That was fun. The two oldest ones would choose sides so that we'd have the same amount on each side. If not, we'd let them play anyway, maybe one extra."

Kay's husband, Ed Fox, had gone to a different school, where the games were somewhat rougher. "A game that I remember pretty well was ground hockey. I guess I remember because I used to like to play ice hockey also. We'd cut sticks out of a fence row, out of the brush, and made hockey sticks from the bushes. Then we'd use a tin can for the puck. Well, it didn't become a good puck until it got beat up and compressed and solidified. When you got hit with that compressed tin can, you'd know that you got hit with something! We'd mark our goals at each end of the playground. It was sort of hazardous to the rest of the children, but we used to have some pretty energetic hockey games. The smaller kids had to find something else to do and stay out of the way.

"Another game we played I liked pretty well was 'Kick the Wicket.' We'd put two bricks at one end of the school ground and two bricks at the other end lying on edge, maybe a foot, foot and a half apart. Then you'd have a piece of bicycle tire. You'd cut a bicycle tire long enough to span across the two bricks. You'd have two teams, at different ends, facing one another. Then you'd kick that bicycle tire as hard as you could. They'd catch it. As I remember, you had to run and tap the brick, I think. Later on. I remember we used to have baseball games. There was a field across the road that we used for a baseball field. In fact, later on after I left school, they organized and they'd play other schools."

Galen Lowman had attended the same school as Ed Fox. He recalled the name of the ground hockey game, although his memory of the rules for "Kick the Wicket" differed somewhat from that of Ed Fox. "We played games together like 'Kick the Wicket.' A piece of tire was put between two stones or bricks and we'd run the bases, like baseball. Kick the wicket to get to first base. You kicked it through the center, while the others were out in the field. You'd kick it and the idea was that somebody would pick it up before you got to first base. If you got to first base, then on to second. If they picked it up they would try to touch the runner.

"And there was what they called 'shinny'—ground hockey. Ed Fox and I were talking about that. We were amazed that nobody got hurt. We would take a tin can and hit it with sticks for a while. It had all these sharp edges, and yet I don't recall anybody ever getting hurt. I remember the expression, 'Shinny on your own side'; if you were over the line they'd yell at you. No umpire and no referee. We policed it ourselves. I don't recall the girls playing shinny. They might have played 'Kick the Wicket.' The hockey part, or 'shinning,' was by the boys. I don't recall that the teacher came out and organized any games."

Grace Knapp had gone to a country school where she remembered a variety of recreational activities. "After lunch, we soon wanted to get out to play 'Tickely Over,' or play jacks. In the wintertime we used to play a lot of jacks. A lot of us girls used to knit or crochet at recess or noontime. The teachers did not take us out for organized games, like physical education. Physical education was walking to school."

Several of the schoolhouses were situated next to streams, and the students took advantage of the creeks for recreation. James Clemmer went to a creekside school where the children had a reputation for misbehavior. He was asked if the older children picked on the younger ones. "No, I don't think so. We younger ones were rowdies too, and I was one of them because I went with my uncle who was four and one-half years older and in the same school. The Tohickon Creek ran by our school back there and we had to walk about the length of this block to get to the creek, and sometimes in wintertime we would take our ice skates and go skating. We had an hour for lunch. Our problem was we didn't stop skating till we heard the bell ring. So when we got back to class we were five minutes late.

"The teacher would reprimand us, take away our recess periods or something or other and we would have to write, 'I will not go down to the creek,' about five hundred times. Me being the youngest, it took me longer to write my five hundred so I lost about four days of recess time until I got my punishment paid for. I probably went again anyway.

"We had to make up our own games; the teacher never interfered. Sometimes there would be squabbles or some fights, but they were over that quick. We would play a game called 'Tickeley Over' where we threw a ball over the school. We were lucky because next to our school there was a farmer who had a field of clover and we could play baseball there. The girls would play with fellows sometimes, the seventh- and eighth-grade girls. Also the country boys had a game they called football, but it wasn't actually football, it was actually soccer. I don't know if the girls joined us in that or not. The little kids formed their own groups."

Woodrow Barringer attended the same school a decade later. He candidly recalled some "play" that was more erotic. The school had an enrollment of more than fifty students, and the relationships between the older boys and girls became overheated.

"I got a bright idea. We had a fence down back of the schoolhouse to separate the farm field and the school yard, a wooden rail fence. One lunchtime after the lunch was et [sic] we'd go back of the schoolhouse where the girls got worked over. All but one, and she got p.o.'ed about it. The teacher passed her house every morning on the way coming to school, so one morning she went out and told him what was going on back of the schoolhouse. Whoo-hoo! It was more than just kissing. They were playing with each other.

"The next thing we knew, we had the school board at the school. We didn't get home till after five that night. They chewed us out for good. And the punishment would be—that was right after the snow went away—we wasn't [sic] allowed on the school playground. We went to school in the morning and that was it. No more on the school ground for the rest of the year. And that wasn't the end of it. A couple of them [sic] students went home and told the parents about it [the punishment] and they went to the school board meeting in a hurry! So that punishment didn't work. So they done [sic] away with that. But the gang didn't dare go back of the schoolhouse again for the school term.

"The girl that told was on the uppity side. She was heavy and always thought she was better than the rest of us. So nobody catered to her. It was mostly the seventh- and eighth-grade students, but a few from the sixth grade were involved in it. There was no further punishment. Some of them got reprimanded at home worse than they did at school. That more or less broke it up though there were still a few of them got around it. We done [sic] it openly right out on the school ground instead of back of the school. They'd watch where the teacher was. He had fifty-two to fifty-five kids to handle."

There were no school nurses in case of injury while the children played at recess or during the lunch hour. Melva Endean had an accident at school and had to wait until she got home for attention. "At recess they had different groups. Some would play hide-and-seek, or hopscotch, or baseball or 'wally-over.' One day I came home with a swollen eye. We were playing baseball and I got too close to the bat, and I had to walk all the way home."

Clara Willauer Kipp attended a one-room school, then became a teacher. We asked what children would do if they came to school early. "We were all glad to stay outside, unless it was cold. Then we would come in. In bad weather for recess we stayed inside or on the great big porch they had on the outside. We played 'Pussy in the Corner.' You had one person that didn't have a corner, and the center person would call 'Pussy wants a corner,' and then everyone would scramble from one post to the other. I don't remember the teacher coming out to organize games. I remember playing baseball. Yes, the older girls played baseball with the fellows."

Florence Vogt went to country school during the 1940s. By then her school had some equipment. "The only sport activity we had was of course baseball. The boys and the girls played it together. They had swings and sliding boards and something like what we call today monkey bars to climb on. The teacher would come out and help, but not always. It was eight grades all in one room so the bigger ones would sort of take care of the smaller ones and supervise their play. I don't think there was too much picking on the younger ones. I can't recall that."

Anna Neamand was a respected teacher who completed her career in secondary education after several years of teaching in a country school during the 1930s. The following is part of a talk she gave at a homecoming of the Richland One-Room School Historical Society in Bucks Country, Pennsylvania,   in 1986. It illustrates the way that the teachers combined fun and learning.

"We had sleigh rides. You don't hear of many of those anymore. We visited another school. I don't believe Mrs. Fluck [another teacher] and I missed many winters in that six-year period that we didn't interchange sleigh rides. We had a geography bee and arithmetic bee and a spelling bee, one on different days, but that was the purpose of the sleigh ride. We went to Mrs. Strunk's school, too. So those were happy days.

"We had no snow days. When we had a snow storm the teacher stayed in a home near the school. I stayed with the Sames and the Shaffers. It was too bad to go home, but it wasn't too bad to go sledding up on Sliffer's Hill. So every night I went with a gang to go sledding, although I couldn't get home.

"My school was fortunate. We had a nice decline or slight hill that went from Wimmer's School all the way to the old railroad track. We had one winter in which we had severe ice storms. I think for three weeks we went sledding every noon. We could take two round-trips down to the railroad tracks before it was time for school. I have a picture of it at home. Sleds on the school porch, twenty-eight. Mine was there too."

In Chapter 2, we included a story by Carrie Horne. We have included her recollections of schoolhouse and school yard games in this section. She taught in a two-room school, teaching seventh- and eighth-graders.

"When the weather was bad and you had to have the youngsters indoors, you better be busy planning to find something to do for them or else you'd have bedlam. We had games we enjoyed together, very, very much, some games in which all the children could participate. One of our favorites was 'Stir the Soup.' Did you ever play 'Stir the Soup'? Well, it's a little bit like that game called 'Musical Chairs.' Someone was in the corner, usually it was the teacher because

I figured that the thing to do was to get out of the way of things. With a baseball bat I would go around and around and around and stir the soup. All of the youngsters would go marching around and around the desks, and suddenly I would bang the bat down hard and everybody would have to find a seat, and of course every time there was one seat less because we blocked one off. That was one of our favorite games.

"I tried to have individual things for them to do, such as picture puzzles for them to put together, or checkers. Children loved to play checkers. They had a number of checker sets, so one day I conceived the idea of a checker tournament. I insisted that everyone, whether they could play checkers or not, would be paired up with someone. We kept a listing on the blackboard. We had the winners play winners, and the losers play losers until they were finally eliminated. Finally we had one boy who beat everybody and he was champion. I had bought a fancy folding checkerboard. That was his prize. I talked with his mother some time ago and she still remembered when he won that prize.

"Oh, we had spelling bees. We had arithmetic bees. A long time ago when I went to school as a student one of the big things was sleigh rides in the wintertime. I remember when I went to school, not in the time that I taught, but when I was going to school we went on a sleigh ride. We had to get maybe two farmers who had big-bodied sleds and horses. We would have two of those. We would get into them and we would go visit another school. We'd either put on a program or have some kind of a match with the other school, and then come back. Sometimes, too, we would have a school visit us. Always we had horns and bells and all kinds of things to make a noise. Luckily, it was all farm horses, and they didn't seem to mind. That was one of the winter diversions.

"When I taught we did have another game in wintertime called 'Snow Ring Tag.' We left the one field to the side of the school unmarked by any other footprints. Then, when a group of the youngsters came, they would start off and make a big circle, one following the other and tread down a path. Then they would make cross paths. Sometimes just two sets of cross paths, sometimes more than that. Then they played tag, but the center of the circle was base. They were safe if they were in there, otherwise no running across anywhere. You had to go around. I got talked into playing with them a couple of times, and of course I couldn't compete with the youngsters, so there was always someone kind enough to the teacher to let her tag them.

"As far as snowball throwing was concerned, it was a problem because we had a lot of kids. We got together and decided that we would have to make a rule. 'No snowballs except in one area, a little section to the south of the school. Only in that area are you allowed to throw snowballs. Now if you go down there and are hit by a snowball it's your own fault. Don't come crying that someone hit you with a snowball. You were in there, ready to take it.' That worked out very, very well."

Commentary

Games were more than recreation, they were an aspect of the "hidden curriculum" of schools in general in the first six decades of the twentieth century, where, as we have found in the comments of some of the students in the country

Horse and sled, Wimmer's School, 1941. Sometimes the children visited other schools for contests when there was heavy snow. A local farmer provided his horse and sled for the excursion. Photo reproduced courtesy of Miss Anna Neamand.

schools, the one-room school did provide opportunities for play that was less sex segregated, where males and females participated together. But there were also games that were considered too rough for girls and other games that girls could play only at the risk of being called "tomboys."

Time was fairly flexible, also. If the students were having a great deal of fun sledding or skating, the teacher might add an extra ten minutes to the lunch period. But woe be unto the student who took the extra time on his or her own, as James Clemner learned when he was punished for tardiness when he failed to return on time during the time allotted for the lunch period.

Creative teachers, such as Florence Fluck, Laura Strunk, and Anna Neamand, found ways to combine fun with learning, as they arranged for visitations by sleigh rides to neighboring schools and friendly competition in spelling, arithmetic, math, and in sports.

Perhaps the most admirable contribution to the creativity of the students was their capacity to adapt their games to the space available. They were also able to invent new ways of using the space and objects in the school yard. For Mabel Foellner's students at Revere, "Kick the Wickie" was a novel way to play hide-and-seek. For Galen Lowman and Marvin Rosenberger's classmates at different schools, "Kick the Wicket" was a way of adapting a game something like baseball to the limited space of the playground.

Children got along together with minimal supervision from the teacher. There apparently was little bullying; the students found informal ways of achieving fairness and adherence to the rules, as Galen Lowman mentioned in his description of "Shinny." Despite the positive stories that were told by many of the former students about idyllic times spent in healthy activities, there was a possible dark side. It seems that most teachers gave little supervision to the outside play activities during recess and the lunch period. It is understandable that teachers needed time to withdraw from the busy pace of the instructional day to correct papers or just relax when the students were outside and playing. Most students responded well to the opportunities for unsupervised play. But all was not positive. As we learned from an interview with one of the students in a school with a very large student population, there were children who took advantage of the lack of adult supervision.

As reported by Carrie Horne, the teacher's fear in the isolated schools was that there would be a serious accident or illness, as there were no telephones in the school buildings, and doctors' offices or hospitals were generally far away. One of the authors suffered a loose tooth, which he did not report to the teacher or his parents, that eventually died. On the school playground of today the incident would have been reported and first-aid would have been available from a school nurse. Overall, those who were interviewed remembered the games they played with extraordinary clarity. Games were an important and memorable part of the country school experience. They provided opportunities for creativity, informal leadership, and skills of negotiation.

"BEES"

> Ralph spelled the word slowly and correctly, and the conquered champion sat down in confusion. The excitement was so great for some minutes that the spelling was suspended.
> —Edward Eggleston (*The Hoosier School-Master*, 1881, 50)

In the terminology of the one-room school, a "bee" was an academic competition. It was most often used in spelling, but could be adapted to almost any academic area. Teams would be assembled on two sides of the room. Sometimes two older students would be captains who would "choose up sides" for their teams. In other cases the teacher would select the members of the teams. A typical format for a spelling bee would be for the teacher to ask the student who was first in line to spell a word from the spelling list. If that student missed, a member of the other team would have a chance to spell the word. When a student misspelled a word, he or she was "out," and sat down. The last person standing was the winner. Students, particularly those who were good spellers, enjoyed the competition of spelling bees. Just as they were stimulated by the competition of games on the playground, they enjoyed the competition within the schoolroom.

Sometimes teachers would use variations to interject competition within the specific classes. Instead of two teams, if there were three or more children within a specific class, the teacher might have the students line up and spell orally. The person who missed a word would go to the end of the line. In some schools this strategy was called "trapping." Trapping could be applied in the math classes, as well. Kay Lowman described trapping in arithmetic. "We used to trap. For instance, in arithmetic, if you didn't know the answer, the next person would go ahead of you if he or she got the answer right."

Spelling or math bees were more exciting if the competition would be between schools. Particularly when the snows were heavy and a neighboring farmer would be willing to take a school full of children to another school, teachers from the two schools would arrange for a visitation and competition. Ruth

Clemmer Giering recalled these occasions. "The best things were the sleigh rides. We went for spelling bees and things like that. I thought they were really terrific. We had recess and went out and played together. Everybody was really happy. We went to different schools on those spelling bees and I think it really helped you, because you tried to be a winner for your school."

James Clemmer recalled Friday afternoons, which often included literary programs. "Every Friday afternoon was different, more like relaxing. We'd either have a spelling bee or arithmetic match at the board, racing two teams. Sometimes we would have other schools come and you had a spelling match and when they got over, you had to name different cities, like if I would say 'Allentown,' and that ended with an 'n' you had to think of a city or state that began with the last letter. Friday afternoon was a diversionary afternoon."

Strategies were developed to compete in geography bees. Mabel Foellner told about the strategy that her teacher had taught the students. "Our teacher taught us a trick, and we always won. Take the name, 'Ferndale,' which ends with an 'e.' The next place had to begin with an 'e.' Of course, if anybody repeated a name that had been given, you were out. Well, we got to the point where she had taught us that we should take names like 'Sussex.' We always won. We learned about a place pronounced 'Shigu.' You only needed one like that in a game to stump the other school."

Galen Lowman recalled a spelling bee competition with another school. "When there was snow we visited a neighboring school, the Shelly School. Mr. Landis took us by horse and sleigh. Of course we had contests. That particular day was a spelling bee. Mrs. Strunk said, 'We're going to have a contest. We'll have the upper grades. eighth, seventh, and sixth.' Then she said, 'Let's make it fifth, also.' I was considered to be in the fifth grade. I got to the end of the line. So, the contest progressed. There were two eighth-grade girls left standing on the Shelly School, but I was the only one left from Shaw's School. I was the youngest one. One of the girls missed a word, and, of course, she was eliminated. The other girl missed the word, 'oriole,' and I won the contest. At nine years of age."

Mr. Lowman recalled these details in 1986. The contest had taken place about sixty years previously in the 1920s. He explained his interest in spelling, which led him to a lifetime of competitions in spelling. At the time of this writing, he was a state spelling champion contender for the American Association of Retired Persons. He felt that his competence in spelling was stimulated in the classroom of the one-room school.

"I had the knack for spelling, and I was interested in it. With the fact that eight grades were in one room, while we were supposed to be in the back of the room studying, the others were supposed to be up front reciting. I was in the second grade, and the eighth-grade class had a spelling test. So instead of doing what I was supposed to do I wrote down the words from the eighth-grade test. I spelled several of the words correctly. I was only seven years old, and I was interested in spelling the words from the higher grades."

In addition to the informal contests between schools, there was a formal competition in spelling in the county. Evelyn Hendricks Potter recalled how her teacher, Mrs. Keller, helped one of the students from a family that did not have much money.

"In those days you had spelling bees. In all of Bucks County, each township would have a representative. The girl who was valedictorian in the class ahead of me was a very good speller, but they were, oh, so poor. She had the worst clothes; and they didn't have deodorants in those days. But it was Mrs. Keller that saw that she had a nice dress to go down to the contest. I think maybe it was my parents who supplied the money for that. There were a lot of poor people in those days, from 1927–34."

Kay Fox recalled a special occasion in her school. "On a Friday afternoon, if we wanted to get out early, we would dispense with schoolwork. The two oldest girls, my girlfriend and I, in eighth grade, we'd have a spelling bee. We chose sides, so many on each side. The side that won would make a square out of their hands, and the one who won would sit on those hands and they would carry us home. They'd go all the way home on those hands. That was really cute. We lived about a quarter mile from the school. And of course I wasn't very heavy then. A skinny kid, you know. You felt real proud."

Commentary

The memories of these academic competitions were so vivid that it was clear that these were still important events in the lives of the elderly people who were interviewed. They provide many insights to the educational progress of the students and to the value of competition in the academic areas.

Contests were a break from the usual methodology of recitation. They gave recognition to winners for academic competence. In spelling there were county and regional contests. School boards provided cash prizes for champion spellers and paid for the transportation of the teacher and the top students from the township at the county competition.

The insights of Galen Lowman are particularly interesting. His teacher, Mrs. Strunk, became well aware of his unusual precocity in spelling and made sure that he was in competition with the older students when he was in the fifth grade.

PENNSYLVANIA GERMAN

> Some two per cent of the children could not talk English! They were Dutchmen, like me; they would speak in the Pennsylvania Dutch dialect and I would try to teach them English.
> —Alice D. Rinehart, quoting a teacher from Berks County, Pennsylvania (*Mortals in the Immortal Profession*, 1983, 181)

No history of school experiences in the southeastern counties of Pennsylvania would be complete without mention of its ethnic heritage. The region of southeastern Pennsylvania where most of our interviewees attended country schools was originally settled by both English and Pennsylvania Dutch (more properly Pennsylvania Germans, as they migrated mainly from the Palatinate region of the Rhine Valley, a German-speaking region). Well into the twentieth century most of the region could be considered to be a bilingual society, as many residents, particularly in the farm areas, still spoke Pennsylvania Dutch. (When there are references to the cultural background of the people, "Pennsylvania German" will be used. When there are references to the language, "Pennsylvania Dutch" will be used.)

Pennsylvania was among the first states to enact legislation providing for universal public schools. Many of the rural townships of Bucks, Montgomery, Lehigh, and Northampton Counties had been unwilling to accept the provisions of the Free School Act of 1834, which provided a state grant to townships that made schools available to all children. Although some Pennsylvania Germans felt that much book education was unnecessary for farm children, and others were reluctant to send their children to school if they were needed to work at home, a major reason for the resistance of the Pennsylvania Germans to public education was a fear that public schools, with their instruction in English and compulsory attendance, would eventually eliminate the Pennsylvania Dutch dialect and eventually, Pennsylvania German culture would also be gone, for culture and language are closely intertwined (Leight, 1984).

We found that there were some cases, which will be noted below, where the teacher discouraged children from speaking Pennsylvania Dutch. There was also a subtle prejudice that was felt by the country children to avoid speaking Pennsylvania Dutch. Earlier, we had quoted Paul Bryan, who was telling about his transition to high school. "You didn't talk Pennsylvania Dutch, because you were sort of ashamed of it. But now in later life, it's exactly turned around. The town people want to be country people, and they want to learn Pennsylvania Dutch," he felt.

Mr. Bryan noted a cultural phenomenon that had taken place in his part of the world. What had been a fertile dairy farming region was becoming suburbanized, and homes in the country were highly prized. Particularly in his home area of Bedminster Township, wealthy individuals from Philadelphia and New York, including well-known figures from professional sports and entertainment, had moved into the township. Many had purchased working farms, converted them to gentlemen farms, and were living in renovated farmhouses.

During the fifty years between Mr. Bryan's high school days and the interview, Pennsylvania Dutch had almost completely died out as a useful language in Upper Bucks County. But now there were being established Pennsylvania German culture centers that are motivated to preserve the culture. An older generation of Pennsylvania Dutch–speaking individuals were offering noncredit evening school courses in local high schools, which were well received.

However, many of the older persons whom we interviewed were raised in homes in which Pennsylvania Dutch was still spoken. They recalled experiences of going to school where English was the language of instruction. Most recalled an easy transition to English and an awareness in the home that the generation raised in the twentieth century would need to be competent in English.

Harold Koder did well in the country school, graduating at the age of twelve. He then completed high school when he was just sixteen. When old enough, he taught in country schools. He recalled his language background when he went to the country school as a child. "My parents were German, Pennsylvania Dutch. They spoke Pennsylvania Dutch at home. When it was time for my twin brother and me to go to school, beforehand, they started to speak English, so we'd get a little of it.

"I couldn't speak English when I started school. I remember distinctly I was in school only a short time, when the teacher asked me to go out into the vestibule and get the basin. I came in with the broom. I got the first letter but not the rest. I can't remember that the teacher spent any time teaching me to speak English. I learned by listening."

Clara Willauer Kipp was a member of a family of eight in which Pennsylvania Dutch was spoken. Her experience was similar to that of Harold Koder. "All of us spoke Dutch at home. When my younger sister Mary was born in 1919, my dad said, 'We speak English to Mary.' But when it was talk among us, it was always in Dutch. My parents could speak English, but they didn't. It was easier the other way. Then when my youngest sister was born in 1925, Dad said, 'That's enough. We're talking English all the time at our house.' I don't remember whether we talked Dutch on the school grounds or not. I don't remember what it was like in school when I didn't know English."

Glenn Haring recalled the extent of Pennsylvania Dutch in his home. His German background came in handy at school. "We had double desks; two boys would sit together. I sat with a boy who had just come over from Germany, and he used to teach me German.

"My grandmother and my father would never talk anything but Pennsylvania Dutch to each other, but my mother and father would always speak English to each other and to us. I can still talk it. I'm only so sorry that our children can't. You don't hear it much now. You have to go out to Berks or Lancaster Counties. There you have little children still speaking it."

It was a source of humor among those who were bilingual when idioms from the other language were misused. One example was recalled by Ralph Koehler. His own mother was the teacher in the Central School. "One time when my mother was teaching, my father had come to see her for some reason, and he asked one of the kids to ask her to come out to see him. I remember the boy coming into the room and saying to my mother, 'Your Poppy's out.'"

Melvin Mack, who taught in rural Montgomery County in the 1930s, recalled going to the school board meeting. "Fortunately, I talked Pennsylvania Dutch. One school board I worked for conducted the whole meeting in Pennsylvania Dutch. The only thing they wrote down in English was the minutes. That was in Green Lane. Ten members on that school board, and they all knew it."

Commentary

During the first half of the twentieth century, much of the distinctive culture of the Pennsylvania Germans was fast disappearing in the region of Upper Bucks County. For the most part, Pennsylvania Dutch disappeared as a spoken language. A formerly distinctive ethnic group had been assimilated. Farther west, in Lancaster, Lebanon, and Berks Counties, the Dutch dialect holds on, as it does in some northern sections of Lehigh County.

Doubtless there were many factors that led to the demise of Pennsylvania Dutch. There was the influence of the mass media, particularly the radio, newspapers, and magazines. The language of popular culture, transmitted by an abundance of motion picture theaters, radio stations, and picture magazines, was English.

A hated enemy in both world wars was Germany. Particularly during and after World War I there was a great deal of discrimination against the German language, which led to efforts in many parts of the country to eliminate the teaching of German from the schools. Clara Willauer Kipp had been a student during World War I. She came from a Pennsylvania Dutch–speaking household. She described the only effect of the war that she remembered: "The only thing I remember was about not being allowed to call Sally Kraut 'sauerkraut.' We had to call her 'Liberty Cabbage.' Of course I didn't know what liberty meant. I knew what cabbage was."

Pennsylvania Dutch was always a dialect that was learned informally by listening, not by formal instruction. There were few serious efforts to make the language teachable in schools.

Probably another factor that led to the demise of Pennsylvania Dutch was the loss of the family or general farm. When the farm was a primary unit of production, parents could communicate with children in Dutch in the multiplicity of relationships and duties that a family farm supported. The father could be the agent who dealt with the outside world, and he could speak enough English to transact business, or find merchants who spoke Dutch. With suburbanization and the mechanization of agriculture, the family farm has become almost obsolete in Upper Bucks County.

As our interviewees indicated, the school was a place in which young children who came from Pennsylvania Dutch families learned English easily. Many still retained a spoken accent, as is preserved on our tapes, but they mastered written and spoken English.

CULTURAL MINORITIES AND HANDICAPPED

Although the rural schools of southeastern Pennsylvania were in a region where there was still an influence of the Pennsylvania German culture, most of our interviewees did not acknowledge as "minorities" the children who spoke Pennsylvania Dutch when they came to school. When we asked if there were any minorities in their school, most felt that there were few, if any. In some cases there were references to ethnicity, such as to children of Eastern European background, such as Polish or from southern Europe, such as Italian. There were very few black students in their schools at that time. When we probed further, we received interesting responses.

For instance, Mable Foellner spoke about an incident in which her teacher intervened to help the white students accept a black student. "We had one black boy. In fact our teacher had to teach us to accept people of a different race. She was very good at it. At first the boys weren't too kind. They called him 'Shoepolish.' His mother had died. His father was in the navy, so that he lived with grandparents who were elderly. They ate differently. He brought his sandwiches spread with lard rather than butter.

"But our teacher, Miss Mary Fox, would try to get us together, especially the boys, when the black student was absent. She wanted to teach us that he was created by God, as we were, and even though his skin was different, he had all the feelings that we had, too. After a while the prejudice disappeared, and we accepted him."

Marian Landis also told about a black student in her school when she was in the eighth grade. "There was a boy in sixth grade who was a Negro. This boy was the nicest boy in school. I sat in the very front row. He sat in the second row in the back seat. I would sit there with a mirror in my geography book and I'd torment this poor boy. He would make spitballs and he'd throw them at me through the classroom, and of course, he got many a spanking until the teacher found out what I was doing and I was spanked too.

"To torment him I was just sitting with my geography book looking at him through a mirror. Then I would make faces. Of course he would see. That poor boy! I felt so sorry for him afterward because he got two or three spankings before I got caught doing it.

"He was a nice young boy. All our Negro children we had at school were nice. I don't feel they were discriminated against at all, not even by the teacher."

Robert Tarantino was of Italian background. He went to the California School. He recalled his ethnic and social-class background. "My dad couldn't hardly [*sic*] speak English. He was from Italy; my mother was Pennsylvania Dutch. My dad couldn't learn English because he lost his ear drum and the other ear was bad. But he could speak broken English. My mother spoke English to us. So I had no language problems when I went to school.

"There were cliques in school. We were in a lower-class group. We were considered lower class because of my father being Italian. The Mullins were in our group. They were Irish but still didn't have much money. I went to high school for only eight weeks. None of my brothers and sisters went to high school, so I figured I guess I wouldn't go either. My family couldn't afford it, so I went to work."

In at least one case reported to us, mentally handicapped children did not fare very well. Martha Tarantino reported upon the treatment of a "slow" student in her school in Springfield Township. "We had one fellow who was on the slow side, and the other kids tormented him so. One time it was pathetic. They snowballed him so bad. They all ganged up."

Evelyn Hendricks Potter recalled a unique group of minority students who arrived in Hilltown Township in Bucks County soon after World War II. "My two older daughters went to country schools, but they only had first, second, third, and fourth grades in one room. Pearl Buck's adopted daughter attended, also. I invited the whole class to a birthday party, and this little black girl named Walsh came.

"I was the room mother at the time. I didn't know who it was so I asked the teacher, Mrs. Gertrude Meier. I asked her, 'Who is this little Walsh girl? She was so well behaved and the kids seemed to like her.' Mrs. Meier said that she had been adopted by Pearl Buck, who had married her publisher, Mr. Walsh. This girl had a black father and a white German mother. Another teacher, Lloyd Yoder, had adopted the older children at the Welcome House. The older ones were Amerasian. Through that, Mrs. Walsh came into my home, and it was a nice association.

"Let me tell you, black children in Hilltown Township were just never heard of. They had black families in the Rockhill end of the township, and one little black girl was so smart, just a young girl, and yet when she was graduated from the country school she had to be in the background. I don't think she was permitted—I don't remember it for a fact—but I don't think she was even permitted to attend those graduation exercises."

But others did not recall that there was prejudice against African Americans in the country schools. Lamar Feikel was a student in a one-room school in Haycock Township just after World War II. He was asked about minorities in his school, and he said, "Well, we had some colored people. There were very few colored people in this area. I can only think of one family; there may have been two. We treated them just as though they were one of us. There was no talk of black people or yellow people. We used to play with those kids, and they were just as close."

Rochelle Renninger Boyle spoke of the children whom she met in one-room schools in the 1950s. including neighbors who were boys from a nearby orphanage and friends who had come from Latvia, by way of Germany, after World War II. Latvia had been absorbed by the Soviet Union. These immigrants were middle-class professionals, who were well educated, in spite of having lived in Germany during the final stages of the war.

"We had a lot of foster children from the Community Children's Home. I remember one of those boys was sixteen or seventeen and still in the early grades. But they never gave the teacher a rough time. The children from the home were not looked down upon. I lived just up the street from them. We used the same bus stop. We used to go up to the Home for Christmas programs and stuff. It was mainly boys. Once in a while some of those kids would come up to our house.

"I remember one of the boys in my school was very slow and I often wondered why he couldn't talk right. It only dawned on me within the last several months that he must have had Down's syndrome. He went all the way through sixth grade. Nobody made fun of him. We all helped him. He could read some.

"We had a lot of Latvian children. We had two girls in the sixth grade and one was a superb pianist, and so she played the piano at the programs. They could all speak English. My best friend from seventh grade was a Latvian; she had learned English over in Germany. All of them were very smart, good in sports, very much in with everything."

Commentary

The years of the one-room school in southeastern Pennsylvania were the years prior to the Civil Rights Movement. The ideology was still that of the great American melting pot. The Pennsylvania German culture was gradually becoming assimilated into the mainstream macroculture, as was indicated in a previous section. There had been some immigration into the farm areas of families of central, eastern, and southern European stock, but they were becoming assimilated as well. There were a few families of Negroes, as blacks were called at the time. Particularly with two world wars stoking the fires of patriotism, the concept of "Americanism" to be achieved through the American meltingpot was still strong. The present multicultural movement would have puzzled most rural educators in the first half of the twentieth century.

Since then there has been a dramatic shift in the treatment of children with handicaps. In fact, the only handicap that would have been recognized by most educators in the one-room school era would have been physical handicaps, such as difficulties in hearing or with vision. The concept of "special education" of mentally retarded children was scarcely known in the rural schools. Children who would later be classified as mildly or moderately mentally retarded were included in the regular classroom activities and would have been assigned to a grade level where, hopefully, they could function. Sometimes that meant that a twelve-year-old child was still considered to be a first-grader. If a child was understood to be so retarded that he or she would have severe difficulties in the classroom, the child could be kept home, as uneducable. Children who were severe discipline cases could be expelled by the school board, even at a relatively early age.

SCHOOL TERM

The term of the country school was shaped to conform to the labor needs of an agricultural society, within the limits of school laws. Farm children were needed on the farm during the planting season, the summer months, and the harvest. The school term began soon after Labor Day and generally continued until mid- or late May. School boards had some autonomy in setting the number of days in the early part of the century, and could have school terms as short as 140 days, or seven months. Later the school term was standardized at 180 days. Boards could also defer the date in which attendance was compulsory until after the fall harvest. Usually that was the time of the teachers institute. Once the school term began, there were few vacations. Christmas Day, Thanksgiving Day, New Year's Day, and Washington's Birthday were days of vacation, but there were few, if any, of the three-day weekends that families enjoy today.

Closing the school for weather emergencies was generally within the discretion of the individual teacher. Sometimes he or she consulted with a school board member, but usually the teacher made the decision him- or herself. In practice, there were few days in which school was closed for snow, for the students generally got through the drifts to the school.

Two of those interviewed recalled eight-month terms. Evelyn Hendricks Potter had attended a school in East Rockhill Township. She graduated from the eighth grade in 1934. She recalled the school term as follows: "We went to school from September to March; by the end of March the country kids were out working on the farms."

Mabel Foellner began teaching in the 1920s after attending Kutztown State Normal School. She recalled the school term and her salary. "There was an eight-month term. My salary was a hundred dollars a month, minus $3.69 taken out for your pension. The elementary term in the country was eight months. The high school term was nine months. We started at the beginning of September till the end of April. If the teacher got sick in those days, school was closed. When she got well, then you could go back. So sometimes we would run a little bit into May."

We asked Kay Fox if school ever closed because of snow. "Believe it or not, I don't remember ever not going to school because of snow. I remember having crust on the snow that we walked on. It was that cold. The teacher got there. I think we got there one time with a sleigh, but horse and wagon could go through everything.

"All the time I went, we had school. The snow never kept us out. The kids didn't all get there. But, of course, we didn't have as much work to do then in class, because all the children weren't there in all the grades. But we got there."

Ruth Clemmer Giering told about going to school in bad weather. "School was never closed for weather except very seldom. I know I was really upset. I was going for perfect attendance, and it was bad and I figured they didn't have school. You know, you had no phones to call the school. And they held school and I missed that one day. I felt so bad about it. I missed just that one day that year."

Emma Weirbach explained that she had not graduated from the eighth grade because the compulsory attendance law for farm children allowed her to work on the farm during the school term. She had attended the Red Hill School in Ottsville for all grades. She had started first grade in about 1911. "I never graduated, because I never had the opportunity. I went home at recess when the work started on the farm in the spring, and in the fall I didn't go to school till after the teachers institute, at the beginning of October, because I had to help on the farm. You didn't have to go until after the teachers institute. I missed a whole month every year. I didn't put enough time in so I didn't graduate."

Kay Fox recalled that the teacher arranged for special activities on the last day of school. "About the middle of May we would all bring lunch and we went to some pine forest down near Rich Hill. We'd have our picnic lunch and pick bluebells, and then we'd come back again, and that was the end of the last school day."

THE IRONY OF THE ONE-ROOM SCHOOL EXPERIENCE

There is irony in the fate of the one-room school. Educational experts and policymakers condemned the little schools because they were not modern. Their teachers were not specialized; the schoolhouses were old and lacking modern conveniences; the students were expected to do much of the routine maintenance of the school environment. These were fatal flaws for experts such as Cubberly (1914).

Yet, in retrospect, the fact that the little schools were different from the norm of bigger school systems was seen by those who participated in them as an asset. Having only one teacher increased the influence of that single person upon the values and attitudes of the young students. Lacking modern conveniences was not perceived as a hardship when most of the homes of farm people had few conveniences themselves. Bringing coal and water to the classroom helped to develop responsibility. At least in hindsight, many of the negatives of the experts were perceived as positives by the participants.

During the period under study, mainstream American public education was becoming more and more uniform as it was being transformed into a "system." Tyack has argued convincingly in his *The One Best System* (1974) that the paradigm for school organization was the urban schools, which were specialized, bureaucratic, and modern.

Perhaps the appeal in retrospect of the one-room school is that it was none of the above. Each little school was distinctive, its culture a reflection of the rural life around it. Yet the physical environment, a schoolhouse built on the values of the nineteenth century, was shared in common by those who experienced the one-room school well into the twentieth century (Guilliford, 1991; Rose, 1997). The contradictions of diversity from the rest of American public education against the continuity of the schools as a distinctive institution sparked the irony and appeal of the one-room school experience.

5

Lessons Learned from the One-Room School

By way of conclusion and summary this closing chapter contains a case study of
school consolidation; an analysis of the advantages and disadvantages of one-
room schools versus their successor consolidated schools, as well as a discussion
of lessons learned from the study that might influence the schooling of students
in the future.

SCHOOL CONSOLIDATION

> School consolidation—a means of both cutting costs and improv-
> ing quality—has been the single most frequently implemented
> educational trend in the 20th century.
> —Mary Jean Ronan Herzog and Robert B. Pittman ("Home,
> Family, and Community," *Phi Delta Kappan*, October 1995, 116)

Beginning even by the turn of the twentieth century educational policymakers advocated school consolidation. Major theorists in education were motivated
by a desire to achieve school improvements and greater efficiency. In their view,
rural schools in general, and small rural schools in particular, were grossly inefficient.

Elementary school consolidation in Pennsylvania could be accomplished by
building one school building large enough to house all the elementary children
in a school district and disposing of the small schools. Usually this was not
easy, for people were committed to their local schools. School consolidation
required funding for an initial large cash outlay to build the new schoolhouse and
expanded expenses for school busing. Prior to World War II, the question of
building an expensive new school usually required a referendum vote of the taxpayers in a township, and the proposal was often voted down.

At the secondary level school consolidation could be accomplished by two or more school districts drawing up an agreement to build and operate a joint high school. If a rural school district did not run its own school or participate in a jointure, its students could attend any public high school that was convenient if they passed the eighth-grade county examination and if there was space available in the high school. Their tuition would be paid by their school district of residence to the school district that operated the high school.

The following oral history, which is also a case study of successful school consolidation, is a description of the dynamics involved in bringing together diverse communities into a school system, which was the task of rural educational leaders of the 1950s and early 1960s in Pennsylvania as school consolidation was achieved. The person charged with creating an individual school system, Melvin Mack, decribed the formation of the Palisades school system in northeastern Bucks County, a region that had been served entirely by one-room schools, and the school district in which Carrie Frankenfield Horne taught. She described her work in the Passer School and in the then-new Palisades Junior-Senior High School in Chapter 2. Mack details how several township school districts were brought together in school consolidation.

Melvin Mack had been the supervising principal of the Springfield Township school district, which had several one-room schools. Springfield Township was a rural district that also operated a small high school, so Mack was concurrently the principal of Springfield High School. A neighboring township, Durham Township, merged with Springfield Township to form a joint high school. Mack explained the complex process of mergers and consolidation that resulted in the present Palisades school district: "In 1944 the state passed a bill saying school districts must get together. They offered us additional state money. So, of course, where there's money, things happen. Then Springfield Township and Durham Township combined to form a high school. Nockamixon and Bridgetown Townships did the same thing, and they got more money. Therefore, we had two consolidated high schools.

"In 1946 Pennsylvania passed another bill saying now we must have other consolidations, high schools and elementary schools as one system. Charles Boehm was our county superintendent, so he was given the directive to consolidate Bucks County. At that time Dr. Boehm depended upon local administrators to help decide how many school districts they wanted in our county. So he asked would I take over the planning for the most rural northern part of Bucks County. At that time we had five townships. Eventually the five townships got together and formed the nucleus in 1948 for a merger.

"We had to find a name for the school district. The Palisades were a set of cliffs along the Delaware River in the townships. They were a distinctive geographical feature of the region. The school boards agreed upon that name for the consolidated school district.

"At first we had two high schools; one in Nockamixon Township and one in Springfield Township and we had all the one-room school elementaries. At that time we graded them. They had primary schools of first, second, and third grades; fourth, fifth, and sixth in another; and seventh and eighth in another. They juggled the students around in buses and that's how we got along using the same one-room schools.

"So from 1948–53 we had two high school buildings twenty miles apart operating as one high school. At that time I became regional superintendent, but we were really supervising principals. We had a high school principal in each one of the buildings. We kept the high school kids where they were and we swapped some of the teachers. So teachers traveled in the morning over here and in the afternoon over there, until 1953 when they all got together and moved into one building, the new, Palisades Junior-Senior High School.

"The day we moved, the kids were to put everything into paper bags, which we gave them. We told them what their locker number was and where their homeroom was. They went to their old school in the morning, loaded their bags, and then put them in a bus to come to their new high school. We took the students from the two high schools, which had ninth through twelfth grades, and we took the seventh and eight grades from the country schools. So the new school had from the seventh to the twelfth grades. It was a junior-senior high school.

"Then the next day the elementaries moved from the one-room schools into the two old high schools. So they closed all the one-room schools, except in Tinicum Township, which had no high school. There they still maintained their one-room schools until we eventually built the new Tinicum Elementary School.

"That was a fascinating period of time. The teachers were in favor of consolidation. They were anxious to improve. The school directors were the problem. Oh! So I went to many, many school board meetings around the neighborhoods talking to them about consolidation. They were afraid of losing their power, their prestige. And they were hesitant about how much more money it was going to cost. But, I tell you, if you got in there and got their confidence and showed them that you were one of them in their community, eventually they would come around.

"Then they had a vote. The county had to decide whether they were going into a jointure or a union district. A jointure meant that the five townships with their twenty-five school directors got together and voted and ran the schools. All twenty-five of them. If they decided to go union district the districts had to vote to go together and then cut down the size of their school board. Bucks County went for the jointure. It was hard to get a union district because you had to have a referendum where all the people would vote. So I operated with a board of twenty-five members.

"With a school board that large you met in a classroom. You had to have a written agenda and copies made for everyone. But I was very fortunate. I had no negative votes in the years I was here from 1948–63. There was all kinds of discussion before items were brought up for a vote, but the vote was always unanimous. We had a give-and-take before the votes. At that time, right after the war, the young folks who became school directors eventually were gung-ho. It seemed to be that they felt, 'I want more education for my kids and I don't care what it costs.'"

Commentary

Melvin Mack was the architect of the school jointure that consolidated five townships, each of which had previously had its own school board. Later he accepted a position as the assistant county superintendent of schools in 1963, the year that Pennsylvania passed Act 199, which finalized the consolidation of schools. In that post-*Sputnik* era, larger schools were clearly favored by educational policymakers (Leight, 1984).

One major change in Bucks County school districts was that the legislation of 1963 required that all school districts have a unified system of schools, similar to the union districts described by Mack, which offered schooling from kindergarten to twelfth grade. After the mergers had been completed, the number of school directors in each of the consolidated districts was nine. There had once been more than 3,500 school districts; there were approximately 500 after the reorganization had taken place. After 1963, school consolidation had been achieved.

Among longtime residents there was a mixed reaction to the closing of the little schools, although most people seemed to feel that consolidation was inevitable. Among our interviewees one of the few who recalled that he had been strongly opposed to the closing to the one-room schools was Harold Koder, who had attended a one-room school, taught in one-room schools, and sent his own children to one-room schools. He was opposed to school consolidation. "I fought it. I went to any meetings that I could go to and I expressed my disagreement. I said, 'You'd never be able to replace the one-room school.' We couldn't have one-room schools today. But it was wonderful at the time."

Probably more typical of the response of those who were interested in rural public education was that of Glenn Haring, who had served as a school board president during the time of school consolidation in the 1950s. "The one-room schools were in operation until 1951, when they started building a new high school and also a new elementary school in our township. If we closed the one-room school houses the state reimbursed us two hundred dollars for every one we closed. We had nine schools. I should know because I was president of the Richland Township School Board from 1951–57. It was then that we gradually closed one and then the other."

One of the individuals whom we interviewed was Gene Speer, who experienced the transition. He had attended a one-room school for first grade only in Maxatany Township, Berks County, near Kutztown, during the 1950s. He had written an autobiography while in the seventh grade in which he recalled his early educational experiences. He read to us from his autobiography. First he told about his recollections of first grade. "My first day of school was one of fear, excitement, and fascination. To begin with we were in a one-room schoolhouse with six grades. It was heated by a wood stove down cellar and had a small stage up front. The desks were old and sat two persons apiece. Since there were six grades, the teacher had to take one grade at a time on a long bench up front. While she was teaching up front we were allowed to color or do our homework or whatever we wanted. I remember one day was so overcast that all we did was talk. The reason was that the buiding had no electricity. In some way, first grade was easy; in other ways it was hard. By the time I graduated from first grade I could recite the 12-times table from memory.

"In second grade [in the new consolidated school] it was pretty neat. Among the things they had was a playground, gymnasium, auditorium, and cafeteria, and a water fountain in every room. To me as a second grader I was just thrilled. A sink in each room! There we had two second grades. I can remember they had a kindergarten there too, and I was just so amazed, because they had these sleeping mats for their naps. I didn't know what a kindergarten was."

Speer was undergoing in an experiential way an educational revolution. In just one year he was moved from the setting of a nineteenth-century schoolhouse to a state-of-the-art mid-twentieth-century school. In his new school there were all of the modern conveniences that were already the norm in the suburbs and in the cities. And with a full-fledged baby boom in the offing, the majority of people saw the consolidated school as a great step forward.

Wayne Fuller, in his book, *One-Room Schools of the Middle West*, summarized attitudes at the end of the era.

Perhaps not many thought of the closing of their school as the end of an era in the nation's history of education; nor is it likely that they speculated much about the nature of education in the big consolidated schools. Many had probably been convinced by years of arguments and the blandishments offered in reorganization campaigns that the big new schools would provide a better education for their children than the one they had received in the one-roomers. In any event, they accepted the inevitable and, at long last left their little one-room schoolhouses to whatever fate awaited them. (Fuller, 1994, 124)

ADVANTAGES AND DISADVANTAGES

We asked about the advantages and disadvantages of the one-room school.

Prior to the creation of the Palisades school district, Melvin Mack had been both a teacher in and supervising principal of one-room schools, so he had two perspectives from which to reply. "Well, of course, the main advantage was that this was a social family affair, getting to know children and working with them individually as family.

"If you were lucky enough to have a good teacher who was dedicated, it gave you the informality of working with these children on their weaknesses and you could find their weaknesses much better than in situations that you might have today.

"Disadvantages are, if you didn't have a good teacher, one who gave mostly busy work to keep them busy, that was a disadvantage. Many teachers brought in Sears-Roebuck catalogs and said, 'Color from pages 1–20.' I've seen that. Then they would say, 'After you color them, cut out all the designs. After you do that, paste them on this paper.' Those were the things that did occur for busy work. But then I've also seen other teachers who had a group working over here and a group over there rather effectively. So, if you were lucky enough to have a good teacher it was very individual learning; if you didn't have that then you just had busy work.

"There were a couple of other things. The toilets and the water. The facilities were not fair to children, especially to older girls. If you were a man teacher and you had an older girl student and she had problems, generally she wouldn't talk to you. She'd talk to another girl.

"Of course the social thing was another. All the children they knew were the children of their school, so your friends were only from that school. If they were ever thrown into a situation years later when they needed to work in a large group, the children didn't have the facility to do it. You could see that when the children were brought into the consolidated building. You'd see how they huddled in corners because they didn't have the confidence to go out and talk to others. You don't find that in the school children today. They can function well in large groups. Social is probably the main advantage and disadvantage. Advantage from the view of individual instruction; disadvantage from the point of view of getting along with more peers."

Grace Knapp was asked what she considered to be advantages of the one-room school experience. "There were times I used to think, 'Oh, we were deprived of a lot. But when I think back now, I don't think we were deprived. There were things you learned on your own. Sure, we didn't have gym, we didn't have parties, and all this other stuff that goes on today. But I think we learned the basics. You were grown up at a younger age. You were responsible earlier for what you did. And of course, you had brothers and sisters in school, and if anything happened to one of them, of course the teacher could call you up, and you'd take care of them and that was it. So we all worked together. It wasn't that the teacher had to do everything. We'd all work together like a family.

"When you think back on it today, it was wonderful. There were no special things. It was just ordinary, common living without all the frills. I liked the idea of the one-room school."

Ed Fox had similar impressions. "There were advantages to the learning process. The fact that you had all of the grades in one room. I think you could learn a lot that way. And the rapport with the teacher—it was a different feeling with the schoolteacher. You got to know her; she got to know you. It was more like a big family. I think it aided in the learning process. The teacher and pupil got to know one another better. I think the teacher could do a better job that way. That's my feeling. I may be wrong, because they don't do it that way anymore."

Catherine Benner Bleam had been a student in a one-room school and recalled the help that younger students received from older students. "It was an advantage that you had all the different ages together. I got to help the young ones. The teacher would ask some of the older ones to help them with their lessons, when we were finished with our lessons."

Iola Parry taught in a school near Raubsville, in Williams Township, from 1939–41. She remembered that the students learned to study independently. "All of the children who graduated from that one-room school and went on to high school did very well. I think the reason being that in a one-room school you do a lot of independent study. You have to help yourself a great deal, so that when they go to the high school they're ready for the challenge.

"You had double seats. A third- and fourth-grader would be sitting beside each other and they would help each other. Not the eighth-graders. They had to be prepared for the examination going into high school. The first-graders needed lots of help and this was one of the pleasures of the older ones. They loved to help the little people.

"Like everything else there are not-too-good parts, also. You didn't have the supplies of a consolidated school, and books and all the resources, because you are only providing for this one little room with twenty students. No library. Your books were packed on shelves underneath the windows."

Florence Vogt spoke of advantages of the one-room school. "The older ones would help the younger, and you'd interact more with the older ones. You learned from the older ones. You learned that you had to be quiet when other people or classes were talking, reciting. You learned priorities, I think.

"Our teachers were not so highly trained as they are today, but I think they had more patience. They had to, to put up with all these kids. Life was not so fast as it is today. We just took our time, went along gradually."

Evelyn Hendricks Potter underscored two advantages of the one-room school that others have defined. "I think the closeness there, even with the older ones. They would take care of the younger ones. Another advantage—if you had a good teacher—Mrs. Keller was so good she would bring out the best in the kids. It made me aware there are older people, there are teachers that are willing to stick their necks out for these kids."

Marvin Rosenberger liked the individual attention in the one-room school. "I really liked the one-room school because of the closeness of the group. The class you were in was small, with individual attention from the teacher, even having all grades."

Clara Willauer Kipp compared the education she had obtained in a one-room school with today's education. "I think that I had advantages that today's children lack. You have association with a larger age group, the older ones possibly feeling responsible for the younger ones and the younger ones looking up to the older ones. There was sort of mutual concern for each other. I think they miss so much the way we have them separated today. Of course, it's an entirely separate era now. And then we were a close-knit community in a small area, maybe a mile, two miles in extent.

"I would say we got more character training in the one-room school. Of course, there was more required of a teacher in those days in the way of character and ethics than what there is today, required by the community and by the school board. The teacher had to live up to certain standards. She was expected to. That's not true today. The attitude today is, 'What I do today outside the classroom concerns nobody.' But it does concern. It had everything to do in the way of character building. If the teacher does so and so, then why shouldn't we do it? A child needs someone to look up to, look up to parents and elders in the professions."

Rochelle Renninger Boyle had positive memories of her experience in three country schools in the late 1940s and early 1950s. "You had basically the same friends, your discipline was there, and you didn't have to strive for acceptance. I was a good student; maybe you would say I was the teacher's pet, or something. That continuity gave me a good foundation.

"I have no regrets. I enjoyed the one-room school, all the different experiences—going to the outhouse and the pump. And there was a pasture next to the school and occasionally there were the cows in it, but we were allowed to have baseball games there. One of the boys would go up to the farmer and ask, and so he would let us; 'Now, be careful where you step.' I know the one-room schools were always nice and light, big windows, six windows, and in the spring you could open those—just a good feeling."

Harold Koder mentioned an often-cited advantage of the instructional procedure of oral recitation. "From the minute the first-grader came into the school he heard seven other grades recite and be taught. They learned without realizing it. A lot of the time when they got to grade six, seven, or eight, they had already learned a lot and it was much easier for them to grasp the rest of the lessons which they had not already learned. I think they learned better than they do today."

Gene Speer attended first grade in a one-room school. He remembered his awareness of the older students. "I think the biggest thing about learning in the one-room school was that you always had people ahead of you and you didn't want to goof up because you were afraid of ridicule. I think that was a motivating factor. You learned it better because of the fear of making a mistake. And that's what helped me in first grade."

But Mabel Foellner described a limitation of the one-room school and her own generous resourcefulness as the teacher. "There was hardly any reference material. Some of the textbooks were old. I know we had no encyclopedia. So the first year I taught, along with paying four hundred dollars back to my father for my college expenses, I bought a set of encyclopedias on the installment plan. They were the only thing I ever bought on the installment plan. I felt in this way both the pupils could get help and I would too."

Lamar Feikel was asked what was the worst thing about the one-room school. "Probably the heating. We used to sit on top of the stove. Many a time we used to wear sweaters and long underwear. The schools were drafty, no insulation. Lighting was poor. We had those old globe lights, but if you were three rows away from one, visibility was poor."

Kay Fox remarked upon the positive climate in the small school. "I think the closeness and the cooperation between the children and the love of each other. It was just like everybody was your sister and your brother. You know, it was so different from going to another school."

Kay Fox summarized her story with the following comment: "I really enjoyed the years in the one-room school. The only thing I didn't like was outdoor plumbing!"

LESSONS LEARNED FROM THE ONE-ROOM SCHOOL EXPERIENCE

A front-page story in a large mid-western newspaper told of a little town with a little school that folks were campaigning to save. After reading the article, a few teachers in a nearby district that was much larger espoused their belief that all such small schools should be closed. The irony of this anecdote is that, at that very time, these teachers were working on ways to divide up their school into teams of teachers and students—schools-within-a-school—in an attempt to make themselves small. While they recognized the trend toward making small, friendly, inviting places out of schools, these teachers were nevertheless unable to use this as intellectual leverage to dialogue the shallow assumption that being big means being good. Because such cultural givens are rarely ever analyzed, these teachers were not able to see the contradiction. (Paul Theobald and Paul Nachtigal, "Culture, Community, and the Promise of Rural Education," *Phi Delta Kappan*, October 1995, 133)

The reality is that most public schools are pretty big. School consolidation as a policy has won. Efficiency and equity both seem to do best when schools have achieved a crucial mass in size. Small country schools were abandoned because policymakers in education considered them to be inferior to larger, graded schools. Enough time has passed since their demise so that a reflective judgment may be made about the quality of education attained in one-rooms schools. The comments of those interviewed were mainly positive. The individuals who attended one-room schools clearly felt that something had been lost by the demise of these schools. Of course, those who volunteered for this study probably came to their interview with a positive bias toward their own experiences in the little schools.

Their comments provide suggestions about aspects of one-room school education that may still be implemented in modern schools. Although the little school buildings no longer exist, there are still lessons that we can learn from the comments of the people who experienced them. We could not re-create the one-room schools, even if we wanted to. But we do not have to return to one-room schools in order to benefit from some of the positive aspects of them. Some suggestions follow.

Building Community within a School

As the quotation at the head of this section indicates, many existing school teaching faculties are attempting to create smaller functional subunits within the present larger school buildings by such strategies as a school-within-a-school. This concept has been a strong movement within middle-school education, for example, as is the organizational strategy of teaching teams. Such approaches have merit, particularly if they are intended to achieve identity and community. The vocabulary of educational practice needs to articulate such values as "identity" and "community" and educators should be encouraged to make these intrinsic values concrete in practice.

One of the authors (Leight) is a member of a school board that is planning to build its first new elementary school building in more than forty years. The current elementary buildings, which were the products of school consolidation and the baby boom of the 1950s and the 1960s, are now considered to be old. A 1950s style elementary school with classrooms placed along long corridors is to be replaced by a modern structure. The architect is using terms such as "community" and "learning families" to describe the clusters of classroom that are the features of the new school. These classrooms provide the teachers with the sense of ownership that comes with an individual classroom, which was not considered in the "open education" movement of the 1960s but are planned so that clusters of classes can share open areas, or communities. But even in conventional schools, the goals of a school community can be articulated and fostered.

Multi-Age Grouping

Most modern elementary school classrooms are age-graded. Virtually all of the students in a second-grade classroom, for example, are seven years old, although their academic competence varies. The conventional wisdom is that this form of organization is the only functional way to group students. This practice has become so pervasive that any other type of organization is considered radical. Yet the evidence from the one-room school is that students of various chronological ages can learn in the same classroom if they are properly grouped for instruction.

Teachers in one-room schools often taught students who ranged in age from five to fifteen in the same classroom. By present standards, they were doing extraordinary things, but in their time, their management of a multi-age classroom was ordinary. A good teacher could maintain discipline and rapport, manage the schedule of the school day, and ensure that learning was taking place although students varied in age and ability.

While Gene Speer felt that he was under pressure as a first-grader in reciting the multiplication table before his older peers, most of those whom we interviewed saw the mix of students of various ages in a single classroom as an advantage. Older students were sometimes assigned to help younger students, as mentioned by Kay Fox and others. Sometimes learning from older classes was informal, almost accidental. Galen Lowman discovered his remarkable skill in spelling by listening to the spelling words as they were dictated to an older grade level and by writing them as he sat at his seat. He developed the confidence to become a precocious speller.

Within the present elementary school organization some teachers are implementing strategies to bring students of different ages to learn together. One approach is to have older students in a particular school serve as "buddies" or "mentors" of younger students, and to tutor the younger children in class assignments during the school day. In some cases students from another school building, such as a high school or a middle school, spend part of the school day as student interns or mentors with younger students.

In practice, many one-room schools often did see grouping of students based upon competence or academic proficiency rather than age. A bright seven-year-old might take third-grade spelling with eight- and nine-year-olds. The nongraded primary school, which used this concept, was a worthwhile experiment of the 1960s and is making a comeback, sometimes under other names, such as a "continuous progress" plan. The nongraded primary is an approach in which students of various ages from six to approximately eight or nine are taught in the same classroom. The instructional grouping should be by proficiency rather than by age. In some nongraded primary classrooms the students might have the same teacher for multiple years. Given the instability of the home environment of many young students, the continuity of having the same teacher for several years could be an advantage, depending upon the competence and empathy of the teacher.

LEARNING THE BASICS

The one-room school taught the "three Rs" of literacy in words and numbers, and generally taught them pretty well. But the basics of reading, writing, and arithmetic were augmented by a strong program in social studies.

A basic education curriculum with an emphasis on the tool subjects of reading, writing, and math was very utilitarian. The skills would be necessary when the student went into the world of work, and would be essential if the student went on to high school. But the modern view is that a basic education curriculum, while essential, is too narrow, and an elementary student needs "subjects" such as science, computer literacy, art, music, physical education, and technology education, in addition to communication skills, math, and social studies. The conventional wisdom is that the elementary curriculum is extremely crowded and that curriculum integration is an answer. But however the formal curriculum is structured, this study has indicated that it is important to provide "roots" for young people in the local community. There needs to be multiple ways to foster a sense of identification with the local community. Through the formal curriculum there can be projects in oral history, local history, and family history. As community service projects there can be intergenerational activities, as with the local retirement communities. The strategies will vary with the specific community, but the lesson that must be learned is that the elementary school students need to study and be involved in their local community every year and that community involvement is an integral part of the basic education of every school.

Standards

One of the ideas that will not go away in the twenty-first century is the idea of rigorous academic standards. Ironically, the one-room school did better with academic standards than late twentieth-century public education. The key to these high standards was the eighth-grade exams.

In the rural schools, the eighth-grade examinations were for relatively high stakes. For the children, these tests were a hurdle that had to be crossed in order to enter high school. The examinations were not easy nor was promotion automatic. They also provided an opportunity to recognize the academic accomplishments of the high-achieving students who would be the class valedictorian or salutatorian. The exams gave an incentive and focus to the final year of elementary school. Recall that Kay Fox asked to sit at the teacher's desk so that she would not be distracted by the noise in the back of the classroom as she studied for the eighth-grade exam.

The eighth-grade exams were administered by the county superintendent of schools. This assured that there were uniform standards in rural schools in an entire county. The exams were a form of accountability for the individual teachers. Linked as they were to the graduation exercises, they were memorable enough that most of those whom we interviewed recalled rather vividly the tests, the results, and the graduation exercises.

However, given current philosophies of social promotion and safeguards for students who have various kinds of learning disabilities, it would be unrealistic to require a written comprehensive exam as the main criterion for promotion to high school. But there could be uniform final exams in eighth grade within the current school structure for all regular education students. There is also something to be said for minimum academic competency exams in the eighth grade. Many urban school districts and some states have such requirements. A graduation exercise at the completion of eighth grade in the middle school is also worth considering. In Pennsylvania, all school districts have comprehensive programs from kindergarten to high school but most school districts do not have a formal program of recognition at the end of the eighth grade, whereas in neighboring New Jersey some school districts are organized for children from kindergarten through eighth grade. Many of these New Jersey school districts have retained the traditional eighth-grade graduation ceremony.

Voluntarism

The concept of greater involvement of volunteers in social services is an idea whose time has apparently come. The President's Summit for America's Future, chaired by retired General Colin Powell in Philadelphia in April 1997, to highlight and encourage support of an initiative to involve ordinary citizens in the life of their communities through voluntarism, is an indication of the importance of community service.

Many schools already do well in fostering citizen involvement in the education of schoolchildren, but most could do better. Again, there are multiple strategies and opportunities. There may be formal structures, such as Parent-Teacher Associations, as described earlier, or there may be informal opportunities for parents and community members to come into the school as tutors, for example. The important lesson is to involve the members of the community in the life of the school and to develop strategies so that such involvement is rewarding to the students and local adults. These strategies help to build a sense of community. Schools have the difficult task of nurturing community. They have to achieve a synthesis between the obligation to be of sufficient size to offer a full range of educational services and the competing responsibility to represent a rational geographical region.

Teachers

It is a truism that no school is better than its teachers. As role models, their attitudes, actions and behaviors help to shape the identity and character of the children whom they teach. They personalize the teaching process and the curriculum. The impact of an individual teacher's personality was amplified in the one-room school. But all teachers make a difference. Therefore, there should be encouragement and inducements for those individuals of exemplary personal qualities to prepare to teach, and the support system in schools must be such that idealistic young teachers have an opportunity to be successful so that they do not become cynical and disillusioned once they enter the profession.

ROOTS AND WINGS

> Teachers had an astute sense of how you both ground students where they are and provide them tools to enter more mainstream participation. A friend of mine said it's like giving kids both roots and wings.
> —Mike Rose (in "A Conversation with Mike Rose,"
> Marge Scherer, editor, *Educational Leadership*, April 1997, 7)

One-room schools are gone, probably never to return, although humans have an extraordinary capacity to discard ideas and institutions as out-moded and to reinvent them under other names.

Certificate of promotion from the eighth grade. On completion of the eighth grade, the students took a county examination. If they passed, they were awarded a diploma or certificate of promotion. The original diploma is 17 × 22 inches. Certificate reproduced courtesy of Miss Anna Neamand.

Perhaps the greatest lesson of this study is a simple one. We all need roots, and for the people whom we interviewed their one-room school experiences provided roots. Carrie Frankenfield Horne was extraordinarily lucky, for she could go "home" as a teacher in the same schoolhouse where she had gone to school as a student and find that the environment had not changed very much. Granted, that the charm of the old school buildings and the positive spin on the one-room school experience generally found in popular media, such as *Little House on the Prairie* fuel the nostalgia that is latent in America's romantics. Still, there were positives that were intrinsic to the one-room school. One of these is that they offered a sense of place and a way of building community.

How can we help to nurture roots in a school? There are ways. One is to develop a sense of local history by engaging the students in family history through an oral history report or multi-generational projects in which students visit retirement homes and talk with an older generations. It is not too late to gather artifacts from one-room schools for school museums. Celebrations of the history of place, such as a contemporary schoolhouse or an old school, is another.

But it is also true that children need to be empowered to "fly." The metaphors of putting down roots and taking flight are not contradictory in the context of the education of children. In order to fly, a student needs the kind of lessons of academic literacy, cultural literacy, responsibility, cooperation, and self-reliance that were taught in the best of the old country schools.

CONCLUDING REMARKS

One of the insights drawn from this study is the remarkable shift of attitudes about rural life in general. During the first half of this century the cities were perceived to have the advantages. They were centers of commerce and industry, as well as major cultural centers. They still are, but they are no longer preeminent.

After World War II a wave of suburbanization began, and it continues today. Families are moving farther and farther from the old cities, and the infrastructure to support them is moving along as well. Rural life is now romanticized. The country is seen as a peaceful retreat from the threats of urban life.

But life on the farms during the first half of the twentieth century was not easy. In the early decades, roads were unpaved and there were no telephones or electricity. The Great Depression hit hard, just as the farm family was ready to enjoy the benefits of electricity and indoor plumbing. The little school was a diversion for children from the tedium of farm life. Although the schools were isolated, they were still the windows to the rest of the world. They produced a vigorous harvest of graduates who have done their share in making the twentieth century the American century.

Appendix A: Persons Interviewed

Barringer, Betty. Interviewed by Alice Rinehart, September 9, 1986.
Barringer, Woodrow. Interviewed by Alice Rinehart, September 9, 1986.
Bleam, Catherine Benner. Interviewed by Alice Rinehart, June 26, 1987.
Boyle, Rochelle Renninger. Interviewed by Alice Rinehart, January 14, 1987.
Bryan, Paul. Interviewed by Robert Leight, July 25, 1987.
Clemmer, James A. Interviewed by Alice Rinehart, June 6, 1987.
Dietz, Mary Hager. Interviewed by Alice Rinehart, May 5, 1987.
Endean, Melva. Interviewed by Alice Rinehart, October 28, 1986.
Feikel, Lamar. Interviewed by Alice Rinehart, January 17, 1987.
Foellner, Mabel. Interviewed by Alice Rinehart, May 10, 1987.
Fox, Edwin. Interviewed by Robert Leight, August 30, 1986.
Fox, Katherine. Interviewed by Robert Leight, August 30, 1986.
Gerhart, James. Interviewed by Robert Leight, August 30, 1986.
Giering, Ruth Clemmer. Interviewed by Alice Rinehart, November 19, 1986.
Hackman, Ruth. Interviewed by Alice Rinehart, July 20, 1987.
Haring, Glenn. Interviewed by Alice Rinehart, October 28, 1986.
Horne, Carrie Frankenfield. Interviewed by Robert Leight, August 21, 1986.
Kipp, Clara Willauer. Interviewed by Alice Rinehart, November 19, 1986.
Knapp, George. Interviewed by Robert Leight, August 30, 1986.
Knapp, Grace. Interviewed by Robert Leight, August 30, 1986.
Koder, Harold. Interviewed by Alice Rinehart, June 30, 1987.
Koehler, Mabel Bieler. Interviewed by Alice Rinehart, November 4, 1986.
Koehler, Ralph. Interviewed by Alice Rinehart, November 4, 1986.
Kratzer, Mamie Fluck. Interviewed by Alice Rinehart, November 19, 1986.
Kressler, Harold. Interviewed by Alice Rinehart, July 11, 1987.
Landis, E. Arthur. Interviewed by Alice Rinehart, September 9, 1986.
Landis, Marian. Interviewed by Alice Rinehart, September 9, 1986.
Lowman, Galen. Interviewed by Alice Rinehart, September 9, 1986.
Lowman, Kay. Interviewed by Alice Rinehart, September 9, 1986.
Mack, Melvin. Interviewed by Alice Rinehart, September 20, 1986.

Neamand, Anna. Audiotaped at the homecoming of the Richland One-Room School
Historical Society, September 7, 1986.

Parry, Iola. Interviewed by Alice Rinehart, May 8, 1987.

Potter, Evelyn Hendricks. Interviewed by Alice Rinehart, January 14, 1987.

Purcell, Beverly Kehs. Interviewed by Robert Leight, October 3, 1987.

Reichley, Alice. Interviewed by Alice Rinehart, January 13, 1987.

Renninger, Marian Stumb. Interviewed by Alice Rinehart, November 1, 1986.

Rosenberger, Marvin. Interviewed by Robert Leight, August 8, 1986.

Speer, Frank. Interviewed by Alice Rinehart, July 2, 1987.

Speer, Gene. Interviewed by Alice Rinehart, June 24, 1987.

Steers, William. Interviewed by Alice Rinehart, July 1, 1987.

Strock, Mary. Interviewed by Alice Rinehart on July 22, 1987.

Tarantino, Martha. Interviewed by Alice Rinehart, October 20, 1986.

Tarantino, Robert. Interviewed by Alice Rinehart, October 20, 1986.

Trauger, Amelia. Interviewed by Alice Rinehart, June 23, 1987.

Vogt, Florence. Interviewed by Alice Rinehart, May 5, 1987.

Weikel, Mary. Interviewed by Robert Leight, July 18, 1987.

Weirbach, Emma. Interviewed by Alice Rinehart, June 23, 1987.

Appendix B: Schools Attended or Where They Taught

Blooming Glenn, Bucks County
California School, Richland Township, Bucks County
Central School, Richland Township
East Texas, Lehigh County
Grimes Independent School, Bortz Crossing
Hunsberger School, Hilltown Township
Jefferson School, Allentown, Lehigh County
Kintnersville, Bucks County
Maxatany Township, Berks County
Passer School (formerly Fairmount), Springfield Township, Bucks County
Reigel's School, Laubensberger Mill, Lehigh County
Rock Wild, East Rockhill Township
Rocky Ridge School, Richland Township
Scholl's School, Richland Township
Shaw's School, Richland Township
Shelly School, Richland Township
Standard School, Upper Saucon Township, Lehigh County
Steeley School, East Rockhill Township
Three-Mile Run School, East Rockhill Township
Tohickon School, Richland Township
Tylersport, Montgomery County
Washington School, Northampton Heights (now Bethlehem), Northampton County
Weikel School, Milford Township, Bucks County
Wimmer's School, Richland Township

Bibliography

Berky, Andrew S. *The Schoolhouse Near the Old Spring*. Norristown, PA: Pennsylvania German Society, 1955.

Biennial Survey of Education in the United States. Washington, DC: U.S. Government Printing Office, 1930, 1932, 1940, 1951–52, 1954–56, 1958.

Brim, Orville G. *Rural Education: A Critical Study of the Objectives and Needs of the Rural Elementary School*. New York: Macmillan, 1923.

Butterworth, Julian E., and Howard A. Dawson. *The Modern Rural School*. New York: McGraw-Hill, 1952.

Callahan, Raymond E. *Education and the Cult of Efficiency*. Chicago: University of Chicago Press, 1962.

Collings, Ellsworth. *An Experiment with a Project Curriculum*. New York: Macmillan, 1927.

Conant, James D. *The American High School Today: A First Report for Interested Citizens*. New York: McGraw-Hill, 1959.

Cuban, Larry. *How Teachers Taught: Constancy and Change in American Classrooms, 1880–1990*. (Second Edition.) New York: Teachers College Press, 1993.

Cubberly, Ellwood P. *Rural Life and Education: A Study of the Rural-School Problem as a Phase of the Rural-Life Problem*. Boston: Houghton Mifflin, 1914.

Danbom, David B. *Born in the Country: A History of Rural America*. Baltimore: Johns Hopkins University Press, 1995.

———. *The Resisted Revolution: Urban Education and the Industrialization of Agriculture, 1900–1930*. Ames: Iowa State University Press, 1979.

DeYoung, Alan J., and Barbara Kent Lawrence. "On Hoosiers, Yankees, and Mountaineers." *Phi Delta Kappan* 77 (October 1995): 105–112.

Dunn, Fannie Wyche. *The Child in the Rural Environment*. Yearbook, Department of Rural Education. Washington, DC: National Education Association, 1951.

Eggleston, Edward. *The Hoosier School-Boy.* New York: Charles Scribner's Sons, 1882.

―――. *The Hoosier School-Master: A Novel.* New York: Orange Judd, 1881.

Fuller, Wayne E. *The Old Country School.* Chicago: University of Chicago Press, 1982.

―――. *One-Room Schools of the Middle West: An Illustrated History.* Lawrence: University Press of Kansas, 1994.

Garland, Hamlin. *A Son of the Middle Border.* New York: Macmillan, 1914.

Gaumitz, Walter H., and David T. Blose. *The One-Teacher School—Its Midcentury Status.* Washington, DC: U.S. Government Printing Office, 1950. Circular Number 318.

Gulliford, Andrew. *America's Country Schools.* (Second Edition.) Washington DC: Preservation Press, 1991.

Hass, Toni, and Robin Lambert. "To Establish the Bonds of Common Purpose and Mutual Enjoyment." *Phi Delta Kappan* 77 (October 1995): 136–42.

Herzog, Mary Jean Ronan, and Robert B. Pittman. "Home, Family, and Community: Ingredients in the Rural Education Equation." *Phi Delta Kappan* 77 (October 1995): 113–18.

Hoffman, Nancy. *Woman's True Profession: Voices from the History of Teaching.* Old Westbury, NY: Feminist Press, 1981.

Kreitlow, Burton W. *Rural Education: Community Backgrounds.* New York: Harper and Brothers, 1954.

Leight, Robert L. "Building a One-Room School: The Dynamics of School-Board Decision-Making at the Turn of the 20th Century." *Pennsylvania Folklife* 39 (Spring 1990): 126–30.

―――. "The Conant Report and Pennsylvania School Reorganization." *PSBA Bulletin* 48 (July–August 1984): 4–8.

―――. "Creating a School System: Key Events in Pennsylvania's Educational History." *PSBA Bulletin* 48 (October 1984): 10–14.

―――. "Duties of a Rural School Board at the Turn of the Century." *Pennsylvania Folklife* 42 (Fall 1992): 44–48.

―――. "The First 150 Years of Education in Pennsylvania." *PSBA Bulletin* 48 (June 1984): 27–31.

―――. "Schools for All Children: Establishing a System of Public Schools in Pennsylvania." *PSBA Bulletin* 48 (April 1984): 5–8.

―――. "A Teacher with a Heart: Carrie Frankenfield Horne." *Pennsylvania Folklife* 43 (Spring 1991): 139–44.

Leight, Robert L., and Alice D. Rinehart. "Revisiting Americana: One-Room School in Retrospect." *Educational Forum* 56 (Winter 1992): 132–52.

Miller, George. *A Pennsylvania Album: Picture Postcards, 1900–1930.* University Park: Pennsylvania State University Press, 1979.

Rinehart, Alice D. *Mortals in an Immortal Profession: An Oral History of Teaching.* New York: Irvington Publishers, 1983.

Ritter, E. L., and L. A. Shepherd. *Methods of Teaching in Town and Rural Schools.* (Revised Edition.) New York: Dryden Press, 1950.

Rose, Mike. "The Prairie Years." *Education Week* 16 (March 19, 1997): 36–41.

Rosenfeld, Stuart A., and Jonathan P. Sher. "The Urbanization of Rural Schools, 1840–1970." In *Education in Rural America: A Reassessment of Conventional*

Wisdom, Jonathan P. Sher, ed. Boulder, CO: Westview Press, 1977.

Scherer, Marge. "A Conversation with Mike Rose." *Educational Leadership* 54 (April 1997): 6–11.

Seal, Kenna R., and Hobart L. Harmon. "Realities of Rural School Reform." *Phi Delta Kappan* 77 (October 1995): 119–25.

Sher, Jonathan P. *Education in Rural America: A Reassessment of Conventional Wisdom*. Boulder, CO: Westview Press, 1977.

Steinbeck, John. *East of Eden*. New York: Bantam Books, 1952.

Stuart, Jesse. *The Thread That Runs So True*. New York: Charles Scribner's Sons, 1949.

Theobald, Paul, and Paul Nachigal. "Culture, Community, and the Promise of Rural Education." *Phi Delta Kappan* 77 (October 1995): 132–35.

Tyack, David B. *The One Best System: A History of American Urban Education*. Cambridge: Harvard University Press, 1974.

Tyack, David B., Robert Lowe, and Elisabeth Hansot. *Public Schools in Hard Times: The Great Depression and Recent Years*. Cambridge: Harvard University Press, 1984.

Weber, Julie. *My Country School Diary: An Adventure in Creative Teaching*. New York: Harper and Brothers, 1946.

Wilder, Laura Ingalls. *These Happy Golden Years*. New York: Harper and Row, 1943.

Wofford, Kate V. *Teaching in Small Schools*. New York: Macmillan, 1946.

Index

About the Authors

ROBERT L. LEIGHT is Professor Emeritus at Lehigh University, College of Education.

ALICE DUFFY RINEHART is Professor Emerita at Lehigh University, College of Education.

ISBN 0-313-30919-1

90000>

EAN

9 780313 309199

HARDCOVER BAR CODE